Read to Me
BIBLE
for Kids

Stories retold by Dawn Mueller
Illustrated by Gill Guile

KIDS

Nashville, Tennessee

Read to Me Bible for Kids

Stories retold by Dawn Mueller

Illustrated by Gill Guile

Copyright © 2013 Copenhagen Publishing House

www.copenhagenpublishing.com

ISBN 978-1-4336-80588

Printed in China

Scripture is based on the Holman Christian Standard Bible (HCSB). Copyright © 1999, 2000, 2002, 2003, 2009 by Holman Bible Publishers. Used by permission.

Contents

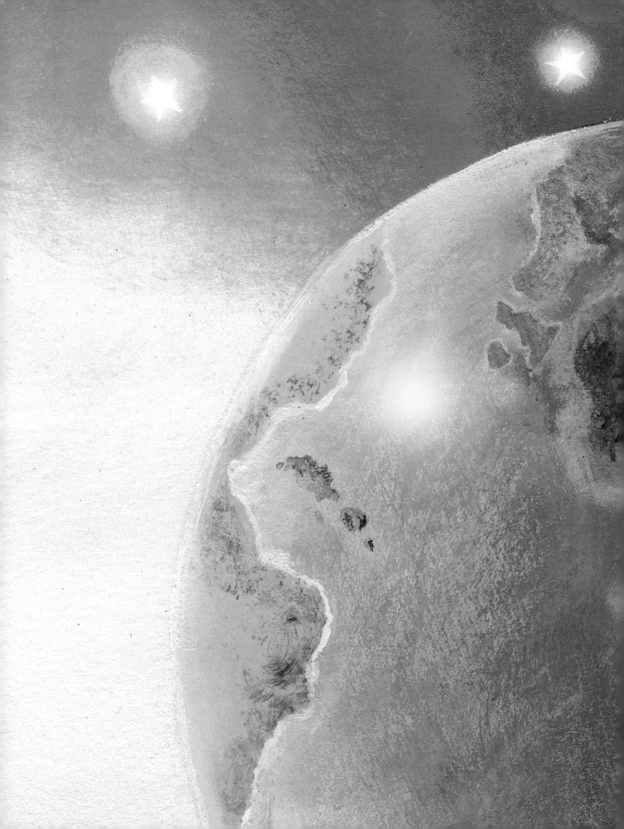

Introduction to the Old Testament

This first section contains stories from the part of the Bible called the Old Testament. It is written by many human authors with the words given to them by God Himself. This book is not just a storybook, but the family history of God and His children. Although there are many incidents that sound like unbelievable fairy tales, they are all historical events!

Beginning with the creation of the universe, the pages of the Old Testament show how God's family grew. When Adam and Eve disobeyed God, they brought sin and death into the world as they struggled under the power of the devil. All people are under the curse of sin, but each generation brought closer the time when God would send His Son, the Savior. God used heroes like Noah, Abraham, Moses, David, Samson, and Daniel to show His love and forgiveness as He rescued His children. These heroes had great faith and strength, but they also were in need of a Savior. The Old Testament contains the clues and promises that God would really send His own Son to rescue the whole world when the time was right.

May God richly bless you as you read His promises for you, His dear child.

God Makes
the World

(Genesis 1-2)

The Bible tells us that in the beginning God created the heavens and the earth. The earth was just cold and dark, without any shape, life, or light. Then God began to create order and beauty in the world.

To make the first day, God said, "Let there be light," and there was light. God saw that the light was good, He called the light "day," and the darkness He called "night."

On the second day, God said, "Let the water be separated with some water above and some water below. Let there be a space in the middle that I will call the sky." The only sound was the waves of the oceans and the strong hurling winds over the waters. The whole earth was covered by water and there was no dry land at all.

On the next day, God said, "Let the waters be gathered together in one place and let the dry ground appear." And it was so. Then God said, "Let the earth be covered with many kinds of plants. There were trees that made delicious fruits and plants that grew wonderful vegetables, grasses, bushes, and the most beautiful flowers. God said, "Let each plant make seeds so each kind of plant will make more just like itself forever. God saw that it was good. And there was evening and morning, the third day.

On day number four, God made two great lights—the sun and the moon. God set them in place in the heavens to give light to the earth, to rule over the day and the night, and to divide the light from the darkness. He made all of the stars also. God saw that it was good.

The next day, God said, "Let the waters be filled with living creatures, and let the sky be filled with birds of every kind, flying above the earth." So God created all the wonderful sea creatures: everything that moves and swims in the water, from the great whales to the tiny fish. He also made all the birds to fly through the sky with their happy songs. God blessed them and said, "Be fruitful and multiply. Fill the seas and the skies." It was evening and morning, the fifth day.

On the sixth day, God said, "Let the earth bring forth living creatures, each according to their own kind." So God made all the living creatures of every kind to live on the dry land. And it was so. God made the wild animals such as lions, tigers, and elephants, and He made the tame animals such as cattle, sheep, and dogs. Think of all the animals that creep and crawl. God made them, too, all according to their own kind. God saw that it was good.

But something very important was still missing! God said, "Let Us make man in Our image, after Our likeness. I will make them masters of everything I have made so they can take good care of all the things I have created."

So, God took some dust, and from it He created Adam, the first man. God breathed life into his nostrils, and Adam became a living being. God put Adam in a wonderful garden called Eden, which God had created for him.

God brought Adam to the Garden of Eden to work it and to care for it. He said to Adam, "You may eat freely from any tree of the garden,

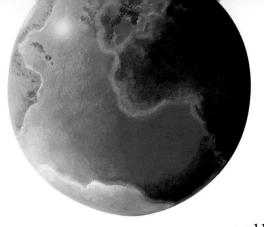

but do not eat from the Tree of the Knowledge of Good and Evil, because on the day that you eat its fruit, you will die."

Adam enjoyed all the animals and began giving each its own name. But he noticed that among all the animals there were not any that looked like him.

Then God said, "It is not good for the man to be alone. I will make a wife for him who will be a friend and helper." God made Adam to fall into a deep sleep. As he slept, God took out one of Adam's ribs. Using the rib from Adam, He made a woman. God brought her to Adam. Adam said, "This is bone of my bones, and flesh from my flesh. She will be called 'woman,' because she was taken out of man." Even though Adam and Eve were naked, they were not ashamed.

God was now finished creating everything. He looked around and said, "It is very good." There was evening and morning. The sixth day was completed.

This is how all the heavens and the earth were created, displaying God's glory and might. By the seventh day, God had finished creating everything, so He rested. God blessed the seventh day, making it holy.

Adam and Eve

(Genesis 3)

God had created everything wonderful and perfect. It looked as if nothing could destroy the happiness Adam and Eve experienced in the Garden of Eden.

But God's enemy, named Satan wanted to make Adam and Eve disobey God. Satan had been one of God's good angels. He was forced to leave heaven when he tried to become greater than the Lord God.

To trick Adam and Eve, Satan changed his body so that he looked like a snake. The snake came to Eve one day when she was standing near the Tree of the Knowledge of Good and Evil. While Eve was looking at the fruits God had forbidden them to eat, Satan said, "Has God really said, 'You shall not eat from any tree in the garden'?"

"Has God really said, 'You shall not eat from any tree in the garden'?"

Eve answered, "We may eat the fruit from any of the trees in the garden. But God said, 'Do not eat the fruit from this tree that is in the middle of the garden. Do not even touch it, or you will die.'"

"You will not surely die," Satan said. He was lying. "God knows that on the very day that you eat of it, you will be just like Him. Your eyes will be opened. You will know good and evil."

The woman looked at the fruit. She saw that it was beautiful and good to eat, and she suddenly believed Satan's lies about how wise and smart she would become. Eve took some and ate it, and she gave some to Adam, who was standing next to her. He also ate it.

But as soon they had eaten the fruit, they were very frightened. Suddenly their eyes were opened, and they realized that they were naked. Then they sewed fig leaves together to make clothing for themselves.

Later that evening, Adam and Eve heard the Lord God walking in the garden. They were terrified and tried to hide from God among the trees. God called to them, "Where are you?"

Adam answered, "I heard You calling, and I was afraid. I hid because I am naked."

God said, "Who told you that you are naked? Did you eat from the tree of which I said you shall not eat?"

"The woman You put here with me gave me some of the fruit, and I ate it," answered Adam.

God said, "What have you done?"

Eve answered, "The snake tricked me and I ate it."

God said to the snake, "Because you have done this, cursed are you above all the livestock and all the wild animals. You will eat dust as you crawl on your belly as long as you live. I will put a strong hatred between you and the woman, between your descendants and her descendants. One will crush your head, and you will bruise His heel." God was telling Satan that one day, a man from Eve's family would fight against him. Satan would cause this man some problems, but the man would crush Satan forever. This was the first clue that God would send His Son as a man to be our Savior.

God said to Adam, "You listened to your wife and ate the fruit that I commanded, 'You shall not eat of it.' Now you will have to work hard all the days of your life. Your face will always be wet from sweat as you eat your bread."

God made clothes out of animal skins to cover Adam and Eve.

God said, "Now man and his wife have become like one of Us, knowing good and evil. We must not let them reach out and eat from the Tree of Life so that they live forever in their sins." He sent Adam and Eve out of the Garden of Eden. Then He put a mighty angel with flaming swords flashing back and forth to guard the entrance to Eden so that no one would eat from the Tree of Life. Now Adam and Eve could no longer walk in the garden and talk to God, face to face.

Because of Adam and Eve's disobedience or sin, trouble was brought into the world: pain and suffering, thorns and thistles, sweat, and finally death. The paradise in the garden with God was lost for Adam and Eve. But this was not the end. God still loved His children, Adam and Eve. God did not forget them and already had made a wonderful plan to get His children back.

The Great Flood

(Genesis 6-9)

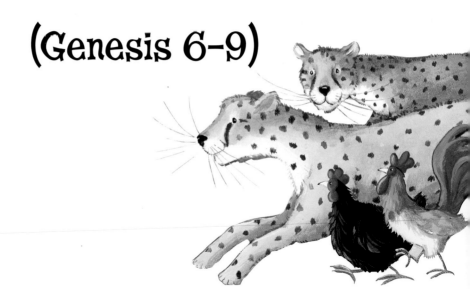

This is the history of Noah, his three sons Shem, Ham, and Japheth and their families. Noah was a righteous man. God considered him blameless among the people of his time. It was known that Noah walked with God. Many years had passed since Adam and Eve were sent out of the Garden of Eden and the earth was now full of people.

One pair of all the many animals that live on dry land came to the ark and entered into it.

In Noah's time, the people on the earth had become very evil. They were mean and cruel to one another. This made God very sad. God said to Noah, "I have decided to destroy all the people that I have made. The earth is filled with violence because of them. I am going to destroy all of the people by sending a huge flood upon the earth because I am sorry I have made them. I want to start all over again."

But Noah found favor in the eyes of the Lord. Then God told Noah to built a giant ark. "Make the ark out of gopher wood, with many rooms. Cover it with pitch, inside and out. Build it like this: 450 feet long, 75 feet wide, and 45 feet high."

God told Noah and his sons exactly how to build the ark so that it could hold Noah's family and a pair, male and female, of all living animals in the world. Noah listened to God and obeyed all that he was commanded to do.

Noah and his sons spent many years building the ark, but one day it was finished. Then God sent every kind of animal to Noah. One pair of all the many animals that live on dry land came to the ark and entered into it. Then God said, "Now you and your family may come into the ark." When Noah and his family, eight in all, were inside the ark, God Himself closed the door to the ark behind them.

Noah was 600 years old when the springs of the deep burst forth and the windows of heavens were opened. Then it started to rain. For 40 days and 40 nights, rain poured down upon the earth. First it covered the streets and fields. It continued to fall all over the world, and then it covered houses and towns.

The waters got deeper and lifted the ark high above the earth. The waters rose even higher, and the ark floated quietly on the surface of the water. Still the water rose higher; even the highest mountains were covered with water. The waters continued to rise until the mountains were covered by more than 20 feet of water!

Outside the ark, every living thing that breathed died: birds and livestock, wild beasts and animals that crept along the ground, and also all the people. But everyone inside the ark was safe because God had told Noah how to build the ark to stay dry and safe.

God remembered Noah and all those who remained with him on the ark. God caused a great wind to blow over the earth so that the waters began to pull back. The springs of the deep had been shut up again, and the rain no longer fell from the sky. After the rain had stopped, the ark floated around on the waters almost half a year. Then one day the ark touched dry ground on the side of a mountain, called Ararat.

Noah sent a raven out from the window of the ark. It kept flying back and forth as the waters continued to go down. Noah also sent out a dove, but it soon returned because there was no place for it to land. Noah took it back into the ark. A week later he sent out the dove again. When evening came, the dove returned with a freshly plucked olive branch in its beak. Noah smiled. He knew that the waters were going down even further. One week later Noah sent out the dove again, and this time it did not return.

On the first day of the first month when Noah was 601 years old, the water was drying up on the earth. Noah removed the covering of the ark. Looking out over the earth, he saw that the surface of the ground was dry. Seven weeks later the earth was completely dry. God then said to Noah, "Come out of the ark, all of you: you, your wife, your sons, and their wives. Bring out all the living creatures that are with you—the birds and animals that creep along the earth—so that they may multiply and cover the earth again."

So Noah came out, together with his wife and three sons and their wives. All the animals, the creeping things, the birds, and all the animals that move on the earth went out of the ark. They were excited to go out into a fresh, new world just waiting for them.

Noah built an altar to worship God, to thank God for keeping his family and all the animals safe. When God smelled the pleasant aroma from the altar, He said in His heart, "Never again will I destroy the earth because of the evil and the sins of man. I will never again destroy all the living creatures. As long as the earth remains, planting and harvest, cold and heat, summer and winter, daytime and night will never end."

God blessed Noah and his sons and said to them, "Be fruitful and have many children. Make the earth full again. From now on, the animals of the earth and the birds of the air and whatever creeps on the ground or swims in the sea will be afraid of you. Now, be fruitful and have many children. Spread out on the earth and fill the earth."

Then God made a promise to Noah and his sons. "This will be the sign that I will keep My promise to you for all ages to come: Look at My rainbow I have put up in the sky. My rainbow will be the sign to you and all who comes after you. Whenever I see the rainbow in the clouds, I will remember My promise. Never again will I destroy all things that live on earth. When I see the rainbow, I will remember My promise that will last forever between God and all lives on the earth."

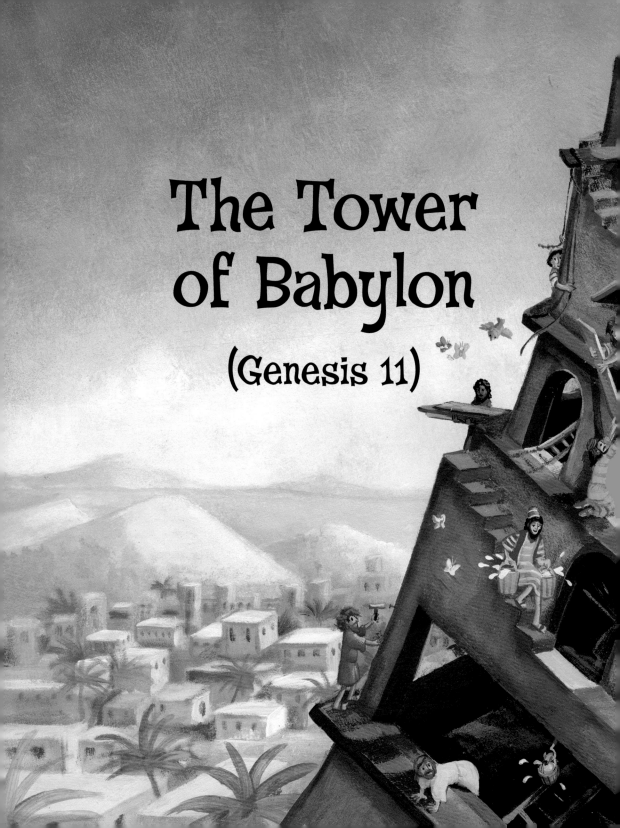

The Tower of Babylon

(Genesis 11)

Noah's sons, Shem, Ham, and Japheth had many sons and daughters and became a very big family. They all spoke one language and everyone was using the same common words. As time went on, many people moved their families from the east, and they built a new city.

They said to each other, "Let's work together and make bricks by baking them. We will build a tall building that will reach to heaven. Then we will become so famous and admired that no one will dare challenge us. We will always be remembered as the most important people who have ever lived on the earth."

But God was not pleased with the proud, arrogant talk of the people. They wanted to bring glory to themselves instead of giving praise and honor to God. God came down to look at the city and to see the tower that was being built. "Look at what they are doing," said God. "They are working together because they have a common language. If they can do this, there will be nothing that will be impossible for them to accomplish. Let Us go down to them and confuse their language. Then they will not be able to understand each other as they speak."

Now, when the people gathered to continue building, the workers could not understand each other at

all. They were confused by the words they heard the other builders saying. They became angry and frustrated with each other and finally moved away because they could not work together anymore.

In this way God showed His might by scattering the people over all the earth. The city with its great tower was never finished. That is why it is called Babylon, because God confused the language of everyone in the world, and Babylon means "confusion."

God's Promise to Abraham

(Genesis 11-22)

In the city of Ur, there lived a very good man named Abram, son of Terah. He was married to a woman named Sarai. Later, God gave Abram and Sarai new names: Abraham and Sarah. Abraham was a very wealthy man and owned many cattle, sheep, and camels. One day God said to him, "Come out of your country, away from your family and your father's people, to a land that I will give to you. I will make you to be a great nation, I will bless you. I will make your name great, and you will be a blessing to others. Through you, all families of the earth will be blessed."

So Abraham took his wife and his nephew, Lot, and left as God had told him. They took all their possessions and their many servants and journeyed to the land of Canaan. Abraham was 75 years old. Sarah was 65. When they came to the land inhabited by the Canaanites, God appeared to Abraham and said, "I will give this land to your descendants." Abraham then built an altar for the Lord. Abraham believed that God would give them a family even though Sarah was unable to have children and was getting older.

God continued to bless Abraham and protected him from many dangers. He became very rich with gold, silver, and large herds of sheep, donkeys, cattle, and camels, yet Abraham and Sarah remained childless, and every day Sarah was getting older and older. Abraham was more and more worried. How would God give them a baby in their old age?

God knew Abraham was troubled. So, He came and spoke to him and said, "Look at the stars in the heavens. Count the stars if you can. That is how many descendants I will give you." And Abraham trusted that God would keep His promise.

One day when Abraham sat in the door of his tent at Mamre, during the heat of the day, God appeared to him as a traveler with two other men. Abraham saw three men standing by the tent. Running to them, he bowed deeply and said, "My lord, if I have pleased you, do not leave without allowing me to offer you some food." The three men said, "Do as you have offered."

Abraham quickly asked Sarah to make cakes from three cups of fine flour. A servant prepared a young and tender calf. Abraham brought the bread, butter, milk, and the young calf, and set it before the three visitors. He continued to serve them as they ate in the shade of the tree. The Lord asked, "Where is Sarah your wife?" "She is in the tent," Abraham replied. Then God said, "You can be sure that I will return this time next year, and Sarah will have a son." Sarah heard what the Lord said. She was listening behind the door to the tent. Sarah and Abraham were very old, so Sarah laughed. She laughed to herself, thinking that it would be impossible to have a baby. God heard Sarah laugh and asked Abraham, "Why did Sarah laugh and say that she would never have a baby? Is anything too hard for God? I will return at this time next year, and Sarah will have a son!" Sarah was afraid, so she said, "I really didn't laugh." But God said, "Yes, you did laugh."

The Lord kept His promise to Sarah. Sarah became pregnant and gave birth to a son. She was 90 years old. Abraham was 100 when the baby was born. They named him Isaac, which means "laughter." Then Sarah said, "God has given me laughter, and everyone who hears of this will also laugh with me. Who would imagine that I would nurse the child that God has given to Abraham in his old age!"

"God has given me laughter, and everyone who hears of this will also laugh with me. Who would imagine that I would nurse the child that God has given to Abraham in his old age!"

Isaac and Rebekah

(Genesis 24)

When Isaac grew up, Abraham wanted a good wife for him. Abraham was now 140 years old. One day Abraham called his oldest and most trusted servant to his tent and said, "Promise me that you will not select a wife for my son from the daughters of the Canaanites. You must go back to my country and relatives and find a good wife for my son Isaac."

The servant took ten camels loaded with gifts and went on the journey. He made his camels stop to drink water by a well outside the city just as the women were coming out to draw water from it. He prayed, "O Lord, God of my master Abraham, give me success and show kindness to my master Abraham. As I stand here by the well, I will say to the ladies, 'Please give me a drink from your jar,' and let the lady who says, 'Drink, and I will water your camels also,' be the one You have chosen to be Isaac's wife."

As he was still praying, Rebekah, daughter of Bethuel (who was the son of Abraham's brother Nahor and his wife Milcah), came out with a water jar. The servant could see she was very beautiful. She went to the well and filled her jar. Then the servant said, "Please give me a little drink from your jar."

Rebekah said, "Drink, my lord." She quickly lowered the jar from her shoulder and gave him a drink. Then she said, "I will draw water for your camels until they have finished drinking." Again and again, she drew water from the well and emptied her jar, until all the camels were satisfied.

The servant watched Rebekah closely. Now he knew she would be a good wife for Isaac because God had chosen her. God had answered his prayer, and now he presented to Rebekah a beautiful golden ring for her nose and two large golden bracelets and said, "Who are your parents? Is there room for us to come and stay for the night in your father's house?"

She quickly led the servant to her house, where he was welcomed warmly. The servant would not eat until he told the whole story of his promise to Abraham and how God had answered his prayers. Bethuel, Rebekah's father, and Laban, her brother, said, "We know this is from the Lord. Take Rebekah and let her be the wife of Isaac as you have said."

Rebekah agreed to leave with the servant the very next day. They sent her off with her nurse, maidservants, and many blessings: "Our sister, may you become the mother of millions." Rebekah was so excited to meet this man, Isaac, about whom she had heard so many good things.

Isaac took Rebekah to be his wife, and he loved her dearly.

Jacob and Esau

(Genesis 25-33)

Isaac loved his wife Rebekah very much. Although they prayed for children, they did not have any. Even after they had been married for twenty years, Rebekah remained childless. Isaac continued to pray for his wife, and one day God answered his prayer. Rebekah was pregnant. She felt two children struggling in her womb—she was going to have twins. She said, "If all is well, why is this happening to me?"

God told her, "Two nations are in your womb. From you, two separate groups of people will come. One will be stronger than the other, and the older will serve the younger."

Rebekah did give birth to twins. The oldest was red, with his body covered with hair, like a coat. He was named Esau, which means "hairy." The second was also a son, who as he was being born, came

out holding on to Esau's heel. He was therefore named Jacob, which means "he takes by the heel" or "he cheats."

When the boys had grown, Esau was known to be a man of the field and a skillful hunter. Jacob stayed back home inside the tents as a quiet man. Isaac's favorite son was Esau, because he ate the food he had hunted, but Jacob was Rebekah's favorite.

One day, as Esau returned from hunting, he smelled the stew that Jacob was cooking. Esau was exhausted, so he said, "Give me some of that red stew. I am starving!" But Jacob replied, "First sell me your birthright." Esau said, "I'm about to die. Why do I need a birthright?"

Jacob said, "Swear that you give it to me." Esau swore to give Jacob his birthright, showing that a bowl of stew was more important than the gifts he would get as the firstborn son.

Isaac was now a very old man. One day he called his oldest son Esau and said to him, "I am old, and I don't know when I will die. It is time for someone else to lead the family. Take your weapons and go hunting. Bring back some meat and fix me a good meal. After the meal I will make you the leader of the family and bless you."

Rebekah heard what Isaac said to Esau. As soon as Esau left to hunt, she called Jacob, saying, "I heard your father tell Esau that he now wants to give Esau the blessing. Now you do as I tell you: Go and get two goats. I will prepare them just as your father likes them. Then you will take it to him so that he will give you the blessing instead of Esau."

Jacob replied, "But my brother is a hairy man, and I have smooth skin. Father is blind, but if he feels me, he will know we are trying to trick him and get very angry." But Rebekah said, "Do as I say." She then put Esau's best clothing on Jacob and put the skin of the goats over Jacob's hands and the smooth part of his neck to make his skin feels like Esau's.

Now Jacob took the food to Isaac and acted as if he were Esau. When Isaac smelled Jacob's clothes, they smelled like Esau. And when the old man felt on Jacob's arms, it felt like Esau's arms.

Isaac said, "Who are you, my son?" Jacob said, "I am Esau your firstborn son. I have done as you told me. Sit up and eat my food so that you may bless me." Isaac said, "Come here, my son, and let me feel you. I want to know if you are really my son Esau or not." Jacob went closer to Isaac. As Isaac felt him, he said, "The voice is Jacob's voice, and the hands are Esau's hands. Are you really my son Esau?"

"The voice is Jacob's voice, and the hands are Esau's hands. Are you really my son Esau?"

"Yes, I am," said Jacob. Isaac ate the food Jacob brought.

Isaac then said, "Come near and kiss me, my son. The smell of my son is the smell of the field. May God always bless you. May people serve you and nations bow down to you. Rule over your brothers, with your mother's sons bowing down to you. Cursed be everyone who curses you, and blessed be everyone who blesses you."

Not long after Esau returned from hunting, he said to Isaac, "Father, I am back now and have prepared a wonderful meal for you. Now, give me your blessing." But Isaac answered, "Who are you?" Esau replied, "I am your firstborn son, Esau." Then Isaac and Esau knew that Jacob had tricked them.

Esau was so angry with Jacob that he made plans to kill him after his father was dead. Rebekah heard of this and told Jacob to run away to her brother Laban, until Esau's anger died down. So, quickly Jacob left his father and mother and traveled to his mother's homeland. One night he came to a place to sleep. He put a stone under his head as a pillow. As he slept, he dreamed of a stairway that reached to heaven. God's angels were going up and coming down on it. At the top of the stairs stood God Himself, who said, "I am the Lord, the God of Abraham your father and of Isaac. The land where you sleep will be given to your descendants. Your children will be like the dust of the earth, spreading to the north, south, east, and west. Because of you and your descendants, all the families of the earth will be blessed. I am with you and will keep you safe. I will not leave you until I have done what I have promised."

The next morning when Jacob woke up he said, "Now I know for sure that God is with me and wants to bless me." He then took the flat stone he had used for pillow and raised it up and poured oil on it. It now marked the spot where God talked to Jacob in a dream.

When Jacob arrived in his mother's homeland, he met his Uncle Laban and began to work for him. Jacob worked for Laban taking care of his large flocks of animals. As payment for his work, Jacob was allowed to marry Laban's two daughters, Rachel and Leah, and became the father of twelve sons. He became a wealthy man and owned hundreds of cows, sheep, and goats.

Jacob had worked for Laban for twenty years when he decided it was time to return to his homeland. He took his wives, his children,

his servants, and all the livestock, goats, sheep, cows, camels, and donkeys he had earned while working for Laban. As he left, Jacob and Laban made a covenant to keep their loved ones safe.

When Esau learned that Jacob was coming home, he sent a message to Jacob. He told Jacob, "I am coming to meet you, bringing 400 men with me." Jacob was terrified. He prayed, "O God of my father Abraham, God of Isaac, You told me, 'Go back to your country and relatives, and I will make you prosper. Please, save me from my brother, Esau. I am afraid that he will attack me and kill me."

Then Jacob sent out servants to bring gifts to Esau, hoping he was not angry anymore. Jacob went ahead of his family. When he saw Esau, Jacob bowed down to the ground seven times to show respect as Esau approached. But Esau was not angry anymore. He ran over and embraced his brother, kissing him with tears of joy. "Who are all these with you?" Esau asked.

"These are the children God has given to me," Jacob explained while each of the women and children came to bow down before Esau. Esau welcomed his brother home. Esau had forgiven him and was very happy to see his brother and his big family. Esau wanted the whole family to be together again.

Joseph and the Dreams

(Genesis 37, 39-41)

Jacob lived with his family in Canaan. Jacob had twelve sons, but his favorite was Joseph, his second youngest son. Jacob had made a beautiful coat for Joseph. When the brothers saw that Jacob loved Joseph best of all, and gave him such a special coat, they hated him and became very jealous.

Joseph had many dreams. One day he had a very special dream. Joseph said to his brothers, "Please listen to my dream. We were binding bundles of grain, when my bundle stood up and your bundles bowed down to my bundle of grain." The brothers became very angry.

"Do you think that you will rule over us?" they asked him. Now they hated him even more.

Another time Joseph had a similar dream. He saw the sun, the moon, and eleven stars. In the dream, Joseph saw the sun and the moon and all of the stars bow down before him.

Now even Jacob said, "Do you think that your mother and I and brothers will bow down to you?" The brothers became even more jealous and angry. From this day on, the brothers decided to find a way to get rid of Joseph. They hated him so much.

Some time later, Jacob sent Joseph to his brothers in the field. When they saw him from a distance they said, "Here comes that dreamer. Let's kill him and throw him in this well. We can say that a wild animal has eaten him. Then we will see what will become of his dreams." But Reuben said, "Don't kill him. Just throw him in the pit. Don't shed his blood." Reuben was going to rescue him later and bring him back to his father.

When Joseph reached his brothers, they stripped off the beautiful robe and threw him in an empty well. As they were eating their meal, they saw merchants riding camels on their way to Egypt to sell spices. They pulled Joseph up from the well and sold him to these men as a slave for twenty pieces of silver. Then the brothers took his beautiful coat and tore it to shreds, dipping it in the blood of a goat they had killed. They took the coat to their father Jacob and said, "We found this. Look carefully. Doesn't it look like Joseph's coat?"

Jacob cried, "It is my son's coat! A ferocious animal must have killed him! Joseph is, without a doubt, dead now." Jacob tore his clothes, put on sackcloth, and mourned for many days. He refused to be comforted by his sons or daughters.

When the merchants arrived in Egypt, Joseph was sold to Potiphar, the captain of the guard for Pharaoh. The Lord was with Joseph and blessed him in all that he did. Joseph gained great respect in the eyes of Potiphar, who put him in charge of all his other servants.

Joseph was very handsome. Potiphar's wife tried to make Joseph fall in love with her, but he resisted. Finally she told lies about Joseph. She said, "Look! That Hebrew slave tried to attack me!"

Potiphar had Joseph locked in the prison of Pharaoh, the king. Even in prison, God was with Joseph. The warden put Joseph in charge of the other prisoners. The warden didn't worry about anything because Joseph was in charge. God gave success to Joseph in all that he did.

One of the other prisoners had worked closely with the king. One night the prisoner had a dream and told Joseph about it. Joseph knew what it meant. "In the past you were Pharaoh's special servant. Your dream means that you will soon be his servant again." Just three days later the dream came true. The man was released from prison to work for Pharaoh again.

Two years went by, then one day Pharaoh himself had a dream.

He was standing by the Nile River and saw seven fat, beautiful cows come up out of the river to graze on the grass. Then out of the river came seven skinny, ugly cows. Next, the skinny, ugly cows completely ate up the beautiful, fat cows. What a strange dream!

Pharaoh woke up and thought about his dream. Then he fell asleep again and had another dream. This time, there were seven heads of grain, healthy and full, that sprouted on a stalk. Then there appeared seven more heads of grain on the stalk, but these were thin and shriveled up by the east wind. Suddenly the seven thin, shriveled heads ate up the seven healthy, full heads of grain. Then Pharaoh awoke. It had been yet another strange dream.

In the morning, the Pharaoh was very troubled. He called for all his magicians and wise men, but no one could interpret his dreams. But then the servant Joseph met in prison spoke up. He now worked as chief butler and said, "When I was in prison, I met a young Hebrew slave. When I had a dream I could not understand, this man told me the meaning of my dream, and it came to be just exactly as he said. I think this man can help you interpret the dream."

Pharaoh immediately called for Joseph and said, "I have had a dream that no one can interpret, but I have heard that you can tell me what it means."

"I cannot tell you. God will give you the answer," explained Joseph.

Pharaoh then explained the dreams to Joseph who listened carefully. Joseph said, "The dreams have the same meaning. God has showed you what He is soon going to do. First, Egypt will have seven good years with plenty of food to eat. But then there will be seven very bad years where no food will grow at all. God gave you two dreams because He will surely do it and it will happen soon. Pharaoh should find a wise, discerning man who can help store food, so the country will not be ruined by the famine when the seven bad years are coming."

Pharaoh liked Joseph's plan and said, "Since God has made this known to you, you shall be in charge of my palace, and all people must obey your orders." He took off his ring and put a royal robe on Joseph. In all Egypt, only Pharaoh was greater than Joseph.

Joseph was 30 years old when he began to serve Pharaoh. During the seven years of abundance, Joseph collected and stored much grain. After the seven years of abundance, the years of famine began, just as Joseph had said. When the people of Egypt cried to Pharaoh for food, he sent them to Joseph. Joseph opened the storehouses to feed the Egyptians and those who came from other countries. The whole world came to Egypt to buy food.

Joseph's Brothers in Egypt

(Genesis 42–47)

Exactly as Joseph had explained to the king, Egypt had seven years of good crops and then the bad years came. It was not only in Egypt that the harvests failed, and people from all over the world were starving. Soon, the message went out that there was food to get in Egypt. When old father Jacob learned that there was grain in Egypt, he said to his sons, "Why do you keep looking at each other? I have heard that there is grain for sale in Egypt. Go and buy some for us so that we may live and not die of hunger."

Jacob sent ten of his sons from Canaan to Egypt to buy grain. Jacob did not send Benjamin, Joseph's brother, because he was afraid that something bad would happen to Benjamin. Joseph was the ruler of Egypt who controlled the amount of grain that was sold. When the brothers arrived, they bowed with their faces to the ground before Joseph. He recognized them at once. "Where do you come from?" he asked harshly.

"We have come from Canaan to buy food," they replied. They did not recognize Joseph.

Joseph remembered the dreams he had about them. "You are spies coming to see how the land is unprotected!" he said.

"No," they answered. "We are your servants, twelve brothers of the same man who lives in Canaan. Our youngest brother is yet with our father, and one brother is no more."

"You are spies. I will test to see if you are telling the truth. As Pharaoh lives, you will not leave here until your youngest brother comes to Egypt. Send one brother to get him. The rest of you must stay in prison until he is brought here." He kept them in custody for three days.

On the third day, he had his brothers released. Joseph said, "I fear God. Do this and you will live. If you are honest men, one of you

will remain here while the rest return to your country with food for your starving families. You must bring to me your youngest brother to prove you are telling the truth; otherwise, you will all die." Joseph had Simeon tied up and thrown into prison while the brothers watched.

Joseph gave orders for their bags to be filled with grain. He had their payment in silver coins put back into their sacks secretly. With food to eat along the way, they loaded their donkeys and left. When they stopped for the night, one brother saw the silver in the mouth of his sack. They asked each other, trembling, "What has God done to us?" As they emptied their sacks at home, they found the money had been put back into each of their sacks.

Jacob was deeply saddened as they told him of the trip to Egypt. "Joseph is no more; Simeon is no more. Now you want to take Benjamin from me also. Everything is against me." But Reuben comforted his father Jacob and said, "Trust me. I will bring him back."

Jacob refused to listen to them. "My son will not go down there with you. His brother is dead. He is the only one left. If harm comes to him, my gray hair will go down to the grave in grief." But the famine continued, and when all the grain had been eaten, Jacob said, "Go, buy more food."

Judah reminded his father, "The man in Egypt said that we could not buy more food unless we bring our brother." Jacob then said, "Take some items that we have grown—spices, nuts, and honey—as a gift for the man in Egypt. Take double the amount of silver. Perhaps it was a mistake that it was found in your sacks. Take your brother and go to the man. May God Almighty be merciful to you so that your other brother and Benjamin may return."

They took their gifts, twice as much silver, and their brother Benjamin to Joseph. The brothers bowed down as they gave their gifts to Joseph. "How is your old father? Is he still living?" Joseph asked.

"Your servant, our father, is still alive and well," they replied, bowing low.

Joseph looked and saw Benjamin, his own mother's son. "Is this your youngest brother, the one you told me about?" When Joseph saw Benjamin, he was so surprised that he quickly went away from them so that he could cry for happiness without being seen. Then he washed his face, controlled himself, and went back to them. "Serve the food," he ordered.

When it was time for them to depart, Joseph gave orders for their sacks to be filled as full as possible and for the money to be put back into their sacks. He ordered that his silver cup was to be placed in Benjamin's sack.

"Go and bring our father to come
and stay with us all here in Egypt so we
can all live as one big family again."

The brothers left in the morning. Then Joseph sent his head servant to run after them and accuse them of stealing the silver cup. "We would never do such a thing. We returned the silver we found in our sacks last time. If anyone of us has the cup, he must die. The rest of us will be your slaves," the brothers said.

"Only the one who has the cup will be a slave," the manager said. He searched each sack, from that of the oldest brother to the youngest. In Benjamin's sack the silver cup was found. They all tore their clothing in grief. They loaded their camels and returned to the city.

Joseph's brothers threw themselves on the ground before him. Joseph said, "Don't you know that I see the unknown? What have you done?"

The brothers pleaded, "How can we prove that we are innocent? God has shown that we are guilty. We will all be your slaves, not just the one who was found to have the cup."

Joseph said, "Only the one who had the cup must remain. The rest of you go back to your father in peace."

Judah said, "Please listen and do not be angry. You asked about our father and discovered that we had a brother. We told you that he cannot leave his father, but you said that we could not return unless we brought him. Our father said, 'My wife bore me two sons. One of my sons went away from me and was surely torn to pieces. If you take this one away from me, it will bring my gray head down to the grave.' My father loves the boy so much that if he does not return, my father will die. I guaranteed the boy's safety. Please let me remain here in place of the boy. I cannot bear the misery that will come to my father."

Joseph was unable to control himself and started crying loudly. He commanded all his servants to leave his presence. All of his household and Pharaoh's servants heard him weep. He wept loudly, saying, "I am Joseph. Is my father still living?" The brothers were terrified. "Come near," he said. "I am Joseph, your brother that you sold as a slave in Egypt. Don't be afraid of me. You did evil to me, but God has turned it into something good." Then Joseph embraced and kissed his little brother Benjamin and cried many tears of happiness. He also kissed all his brothers, and he said to them, "Go and bring our father to come and stay with us here in Egypt so we can all live as one big family again."

Pharaoh was pleased that Joseph's brothers had come. He ordered them to take wagons back to Canaan so they could quickly move to Egypt. Jacob could not believe the news about Joseph when they told him, "Joseph is still alive. He rules all Egypt." His did not know what to think. Finally, when he saw the wagons from Egypt, he believed it was true.

When Jacob and his big family had arrived, Pharaoh, the king of Egypt, gave them a wonderful piece of land in Egypt in Goshen, where they could live safely through the years of famine.

The Baby in the Basket

(Exodus 1-2)

After Joseph and his family had died, their children, called the Israelites, still lived in Egypt in the land of Goshen. But things did not go well for the Israelites after Joseph died. New kings, called pharaohs, did not like the Israelites and forced them to live as slaves in Egypt. The Israelites had to work hard and long and did not have much food. They were commanded to work hard every day and even built the cities of Pithom and Rameses. As they worked harder and harder by the Egyptians, God still made the Israelites stronger and multiplied their families.

The evil Pharaoh was afraid that the Israelites would have so many children that they would outnumber the Egyptians and try to take over their kingdom. He then made a cruel and terrible decision that all the Israelite baby boys must be killed. The Israelites were afraid of Pharaoh and prayed to God for help.

One Israelite woman gave birth to a baby boy. She took care of him for three months but could not hide him any longer. She made a basket that could float like a boat. Then she put the baby in it and sent the basket out on the river Nile. She trusted that God would save her baby. The little boy's sister, Miriam, was hiding and watching the basket floating on the river.

Then the daughter of Pharaoh came down to the river to bathe. The princess saw the basket floating among the reeds. She sent her servant to get it for her. When she opened it, the baby was crying. The princess was filled with compassion and said, "This is one of the babies of the Hebrews!"

Miriam boldly came up to the princess and asked, "Would you like me to find a Hebrew woman who can nurse him for you?"

The princess told her, "Go." Miriam quickly returned with her mother. Pharaoh's daughter said, "Take this child into your house and care for him for me. I will pay you." The happy mother took her son back into her home. She lovingly cared for him until he was old enough to eat food by himself. Then she brought him to the daughter of Pharaoh, who raised him as her own son. The princess said, "I will name him Moses, because I have taken him out of the water."

The princess was filled with compassion and said, "This is one of the babies of the Hebrews! I will name him Moses, because I have taken him out of the water."

God Calls Moses

(Exodus 2-4)

Moses grew up in the house of Pharaoh. Even when he had become a man, he remained there as the son of the princess. But Moses knew that he was an Israelite. He was angry to see how the Egyptians were cruel to the Israelite slaves, so he tried to help some of his people.

One day, as he went walking, Moses saw an Egyptian mistreating one of the Israelites. Moses carefully looked around. Seeing no one, he rescued the Israelite by killing the Egyptian and burying him in the sand.

The next day, he went out again and saw two Israelites fighting. Moses asked, "Why are you hurting your brother?" The man fighting said, "Are you going to kill me as you killed the Egyptian?" Moses realized that his life was in danger. When Pharaoh found out about it, he tried to kill Moses, so Moses had to run away from Egypt.

Moses ran to Midian and began working as a shepherd of a priest named Jethro. He lived there for 40 years, taking care of sheep. Moses married Jethro's daughter Zipporah, and they had two sons.

While Moses remained in Midian with Jethro, God heard the cries of His children in Egypt. God had not forgotten His people.

One day, as Moses was out watching Jethro's sheep grazing near a mountain, he suddenly saw a very strange bush. The bush was on fire, but it did not burn up. Moses walked over to the bush. Just then God appeared to him and called to Moses from inside the burning bush. God's voice was coming from the fire and said, "Do not come near. Take off your sandals. The place where you are standing is holy ground. I am the God of your father, the God of Abraham, the God of Isaac, and the God of Jacob." Moses hid his face because he was afraid to look at God.

God said to Moses, "I have seen my people, the Israelites, suffering in Egypt, and I have not forgotten them. Tell Pharaoh that the Israelites are My people and I want the people to leave Egypt. Moses, you must lead them out of Egypt." But Moses was afraid to go back to Egypt and said, "Who am I to go to Pharaoh and bring the children of Israel out of Egypt?"

God said to Moses, "I will be with you. This will be a sign for you. When you have come out of Egypt, you will all worship Me on this mountain."

"I am the God of your father,
the God of Abraham, the God of Isaac,
and the God of Jacob."

Moses said, "When I say to the people, 'The God of your fathers has sent me,' and they ask me to tell them Your name, what should I tell them?"

God said, "I AM WHO I AM. Tell the children of Israel that I AM has sent you. Tell them the God of their fathers, the God of Abraham, the God of Isaac, and the God of Jacob has sent me to you. This is My name forever."

But Moses was still afraid and said, "They won't listen to me. They will say, 'God did not really appear to you.'"

But God said, "I will keep you safe. Take your staff and use it to perform miracles in Egypt. You will lead them to Canaan to the land that I promised to Abraham. Go now, and I will be with you."

Moses was still afraid, and said, "Oh, Lord, please send someone else."

Now, God was angry with Moses. "I know that your brother, Aaron, speaks well. He is coming now to meet you. He can be your mouth. I will tell you what to say, and Aaron can speak for you to the people. Take your staff, and with it you can show My signs."

Moses went to Jethro to ask permission to visit his family back in Egypt. After Jethro blessed him, Moses took his wife and sons to Egypt. Soon he met Aaron. Embracing him, Moses shared the plan that God had made. Aaron spoke for Moses, and the people believed that God had seen their suffering and that God had chosen Moses to lead them out of Egypt. They bowed their heads and worshipped in gratitude.

Out of Egypt
(Exodus 5-12)

Moses and Aaron went up and stood before Pharaoh and said, "We have met with God, the God of Israel, who has said, 'Let My people go." But Pharaoh said, "Who is the Lord? Why should I obey Him? I don't know Him, and I will not let Israel go!" Instead he commanded that the Israelites work even harder.

Because Pharaoh would not listen to Moses, God sent ten plagues over Egypt. First, God turned the water in Egypt into blood. The Nile River and ponds were all filled with blood. No one could find good water to drink. But Pharaoh still would not let the people go.

A week later, God sent Moses to Pharaoh again. "Tell Pharaoh to let My people go. If he refuses, I will send a plague of frogs upon all Egypt. They will come up into the palace and into all the houses, into the beds, the ovens, and the kneading bowls." Aaron stretched his staff over the Nile River as God directed. Frogs from the river, ponds, and streams came up and covered the land. Pharaoh's royal sorcerers used their tricks to make frogs come upon the land too.

After some time, Pharaoh called Moses and Aaron. "Pray to your Lord and ask Him to take the frogs away. Then I will let the people go." God allowed Pharaoh to choose the time for the frogs to leave. He chose the next day. But the next day, as all the frogs died, Pharaoh changed his mind and would not let the people go. The people put the frogs in huge piles. The frogs stunk as they rotted.

For the third plague, God told Aaron to hit the dust of the ground. Suddenly the dust became gnats which attacked all of the people and animals. All of the dust became biting gnats. Pharaoh's magicians tried to make gnats using their tricks, but could not. They told Pharaoh that this was "the finger of God." But Pharaoh did not listen to them.

Then God sent swarms of flies over Egypt. This was the fourth plague. All the Egyptian houses were filled with flies. They swarmed on Pharaoh and his officials. The land was ruined by the flies, but in Goshen where the Israelites lived, there were no flies. It was terrible for the Egyptians, and finally Pharaoh promised Moses that the people could leave if only the flies would go away. But again, just as God made the gnats and flies go away, Pharaoh regretted what he had promised.

God sent Moses back to talk to Pharaoh again. "Tell Pharaoh that, if he refuses to let My people go, a deadly plague will come upon the cattle, horses, camels, donkeys, sheep, and goats that belong to his people, the Egyptians." The next day it happened as God had said. All the livestock of the Egyptians died. Pharaoh sent servants to visit the animals in Goshen. They reported that all the animals of the Israelites remained healthy.

God told Aaron to throw ashes from the furnace into the air to make the sixth plague. The ashes became dust that went through the air and made painful sores on every Egyptian. The painful, oozing sores covered the Egyptians' bodies, from the top of their heads to the bottom of their feet. People were hurting too much to stand up and had to stay in bed.

For the seventh plague, God sent a terrible storm over Egypt with huge hailstones that crushed every plant and all the crops in the fields. The Egyptians had never seen a storm like this before. Still, Pharaoh refused to let the Israelites leave Egypt. Then God sent swarms of locusts all over Egypt. This was the eighth plague. They came in swarms of millions until they covered the entire land. The locusts ate every green plant that was still alive after the hailstorm.

The ninth plague was a plague of darkness. Again God told Moses, "Stretch out your hand toward heaven. I will bring darkness over Egypt that can even be felt." Moses stretched his hand to the heavens, and darkness fell upon the entire land of Egypt that lasted three days. None of the Egyptians could see each other. No one left his house for three days. But in the houses of God's people, the Israelites, there was light!

God then said to Moses, "Pharaoh will soon let you go. Therefore, go and tell your people to be ready to leave. Each family must gather tonight and eat a meal together. It must be an entire lamb, and they must share it with the neighbors. If any is left over, it must be burned. Eat the lamb with bitter herbs and bread made without yeast. Eat it in a hurry, with your belt fastened, your sandals on your feet, and your staff in your hand. This is the Passover meal. Tonight My angel will pass through Egypt and strike down the firstborn of all, man and animals. I will show My power tonight, and Pharaoh will let My people go. Take the blood from the lamb you eat, and it will be a sign: When I see the blood, I will pass by this house and this family and do no harm."

Moses did as God said, and the Israelites gathered their belongings and prepared to leave Egypt. The families gathered together and ate a big meal, which is called the Passover meal. They painted the blood on the tops and sides of the doorframes of their houses, just as God had told them to do.

On that same night all the firstborn boys in Egypt died. Even Pharaoh's son died. But among the Israelites, nobody died. God's angel saw the sign of the blood on the tops and sides of the doorframes of the houses. God's angel passed over them and kept all of the Israelites safe. This was the tenth plague God sent over Egypt.

That same night Pharaoh called on Moses and said, "I have had enough. Take your people and go."

When they left Egypt, there were about 600,000 men, along with women and children. Many Egyptians also left with the Israelites. The Israelites brought all their flocks and herds. The Israelites had lived in Egypt for 430 years.

Through the Big Sea!

(Exodus 13–17)

Moses led the Israelites out of Egypt. During the day God went ahead of His people in a thick cloud, and during the night He went ahead of them in a flaming fire. That way God could lead them at all times, whether day or night.

On their way, they came to a big sea called the Red Sea, where they camped. But once again Pharaoh regretted his decision and sent out his big armies to bring back the Israelites to Egypt. Pharaoh took more than 600 of his best chariots, all his other chariots, and soldiers.

As the Israelites saw the Egyptians approaching, they were terrified. They said to Moses, "Why did you bring us out here in the desert to die? Didn't we tell you to let us serve the Egyptians? It would have been better to serve in Egypt than to die here in the wilderness!"

Moses said, "Don't be afraid. Stand still and see how God will help us. God will fight for you. Just be still."

God told Moses, "Stretch your hand out over the sea." When Moses stretched out his hand, God sent a storm that blew so hard the waters were pulled back. A wide path opened in the sea, right in front of the Israelites. The path led all the way to the other side of the sea. The Israelites could now escape from Pharaoh's army through the sea, bringing with them all their animals and belongings, without even getting wet.

Pharaoh saw that they were escaping. So, he gave orders for his men to follow them between the walls of water into the middle of the sea. As morning was coming, God looked down from the cloud and threw the Egyptians into a panic. Their chariot wheels became stuck and fell off. "Let us go back," Pharaoh ordered. "The Lord is fighting for them." Then God told Moses, "Put your hand over the sea again so that the waters will flow back over the Egyptians, their chariots, and their horsemen."

Moses stretched out his hand, and the water returned filling in the path where the Israelites had crossed. The Egyptians were swept back into the sea. In the morning the Israelites could see that Pharaoh's entire army had been destroyed. But the Israelites had crossed over to safety on dry land. God had saved His people from Pharaoh's army and they no longer had to live as slaves in Egypt.

The Israelites were now in a large desert where they journeyed from place to place. It was hot and hard to be in a desert, so the people started to complain to Moses that they did not have enough food. So, God sent food to the people in a special way. Each morning pieces of sweet bread, called manna, were lying on the ground when they woke up. Later in the afternoon God sent quails into the camp that the Israelites could easily catch and eat. Everywhere they went, God took care of the people and sent enough manna from the heavens each morning.

But one day, they came to a place where there was no water at all to drink. The people started to complain again to Moses, "Give us something to drink," they said. Moses prayed to God. And God showed him a large rock and said, "Strike the rock with your staff." Moses did what God had told him to, and immediately water came rushing from the rock. Now the people could drink as much water as they wanted. Once again God had helped His people.

The Ten Commandments

(Exodus 19-34)

The Israelites continued their journey in the big desert. One day they arrived at the same mountain where Moses had seen the burning bush. They put up their tents and camped there. As they looked up, a dark cloud covered the mountain. Lightning flashed from the cloud, and loud thunder shook the earth. God was on the mountain.

Moses climbed up the mountain to talk to God. For forty days, Moses stayed on the mountaintop where God talked to him. God said, "I am the Lord your God who has brought you out of Egypt. I have rescued you from slavery.

"Worship God only. Do not make any idols or worship anything else.
My name is holy. Do not use it for evil.
Keep the seventh day of the week holy and do your work in six days.
Honor your father and mother.
Do not kill.
Do not break the promises you make when you marry.
Do not steal.
Do not tell lies.
Do not be jealous for the things that belong to your neighbor."

God Himself carved these laws on two large, flat stone tablets. God called Moses up the mountain to give him the stones so Moses could teach these commandments and instructions to God's people. But while Moses was away, the people gathered together and said to Moses' brother, Aaron, "We don't know what has happened to Moses. Make some new gods for us so that we can worship them."

Aaron, the leader while Moses was away, told them to give him their golden earrings. Aaron used a chisel to make a mold. He melted down the golden earrings and made a calf out of gold. Then Aaron made an altar for it and said, "Tomorrow is a feast day to the golden calf." The people made burnt offerings to the golden calf, eating and drinking in celebration and worshipping it.

Moses went down from the mountain to see the people. He was bringing the covenant of God written on the two flat stone tablets. They were inscribed on both sides by God's own fingers. When Moses saw the people were worshipping a golden calf, he was very angry. He threw the tablets down to the ground, breaking them into pieces at the foot of the mountain.

Moses said to Aaron, "What did these people do to you that made you lead them into sin like this?" Aaron said, "Please, don't be angry with me. The people asked me to make a god because they didn't know what had happened to you. I told them to take off their gold jewelry. I threw it into the fire, and out came this calf."

Moses then prayed to God for the people. Because Moses asked God to forgive them, God showed mercy and forgave the Israelites. Later, He made new stones with all of the special instructions and gave them to Moses.

Moses carried the tablets of stone back to the camp and read them to the people. Moses told the people, "We are going to build a special place to worship God. It will be a large, beautiful tent called the tabernacle." They built the tabernacle in the very middle of the camp. They made colorful curtains for the tent and decorated it with silver and gold. When the tabernacle was finished, a cloud appeared and hovered in the air just above the tabernacle. The cloud showed them that God was with them always!

The Walls of Jericho

(Numbers 13-14; 27; Deuteronomy 34; Joshua 1-3; 5-6)

After many months of travel, the Israelites came to the edge of Canaan, the land God had promised to Abraham, Isaac, and Jacob so many years ago. God said to Moses, "Send in some men to see what the country is like." Moses picked twelve men and instructed them to scout out the land and find out if the land was a good place and to see if the enemy armies were strong.

Forty days later, when the men returned, they carried a cluster of grapes that was so huge it took two men to carry it. Ten of the scouts reported, "Truly, it is a land flowing with milk and honey. See the fruit we brought. But the people live in large, walled cities. We cannot fight these men."

The other two scouts, Joshua and Caleb, told the people, "Yes, we can take the land. God will help us."

But the people were still afraid and did not want to listen to them. Then God got angry at the Israelites because they would not trust Him to help them, and He said, "Because you are afraid and don't trust in Me, you will not enter the Promised Land. I will give it to your children, but you will wander in the wilderness for 40 years. Only Caleb and Joshua will go into the Promised Land because they trusted Me."

After forty years, God decided it was time for the people to enter Canaan. God told Moses that he would not lead the people into the Promised Land. Instead God chose Joshua to become the new leader of the Israelites.

Moses again told the people to remember everything God had commanded. Then God led Moses up to the top of Mount Nebo to show Moses the land He had promised to give to Abraham, Isaac, and Jacob. By now Moses was 120 years old, but his eyes had not dimmed, and he had not lost his strength. When Moses died, God Himself buried him on the mountain.

The Israelites crossed the Jordan River and came to the big city of Jericho. A high, thick wall surrounded the city. But Joshua was not worried because God had already told him how the city would be conquered. Joshua sent out two men to Jericho. They were staying with a woman named Rahab. Messengers from the king of the city came to her house and said, "We know that your guests are Israelites and are looking over our whole land. We have orders to bring them to the king."

Rahab said, "Yes, some men came to me. I do not know where they came from, but they are already gone. They left before the city gate was closed." The king's men believed what she said and left quickly to catch them.

Then Rahab went to the roof of her house where the Joshua's men were hiding. "I know that God has given you this land. We have heard how God dried up the Red Sea for you and how He helped you all these years in the desert. Now, as I have been kind to you, please show kindness to me. Please keep my family alive and save us when you capture this city."

The men promised, "Our lives for your lives, as long as none of you tell of our agreement. When God gives us this land, we will be kind and faithful to you."

Rahab's house was built into the side of the city wall. She helped the men escape through the window by using a rope. The men said, "Hang this red rope in the window. Whoever is in your home, your father, mother, brothers, and all their family members, will be safe. But you must keep this a secret." Rahab agreed and hung the red rope in the window.

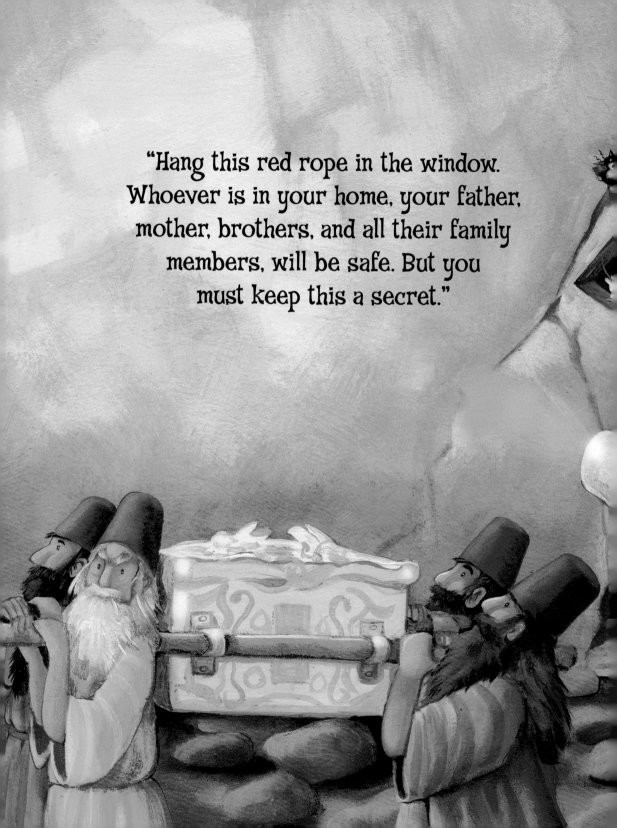

"Hang this red rope in the window. Whoever is in your home, your father, mother, brothers, and all their family members, will be safe. But you must keep this a secret."

The men returned to Joshua. "It is true," they said. "God has given the city into our hands. They are melting in fear because of us." Joshua now commanded his army to march around the city every day for the next six days. Then, on the seventh day, God told the priests leading the army around the city walls to blow their trumpets, and all the people shouted out loud at the same time. All at once, the walls of Jericho fell, and the Israelites easily captured the city. The men kept their promise and rescued Rahab and all her family.

Finally, after many years in the desert, the Israelites were living in their own land. The promise so many years earlier to Abraham had now been fulfilled by God.

Gideon

(Judges 6-8)

Like Moses, Joshua was a good leader of Israel. But after Joshua had died, the Israelites forgot about God. God allowed other nations' armies to come into Israel and steal their food and animals. Every time the Israelites asked God for forgiveness and started praying to Him again, God would help them. God's way to help was to send men who were skilled warriors of great courage. These great leaders were called judges and one of them was Gideon.

At first, Gideon was afraid of the job God wanted him to do. How could he save Israel from its strong enemies? Gideon said to God, "Show me that You really want me to be a leader. Give me a sign to prove it to me."

Gideon asked God, "If you are really going to use me to deliver Israel, please give me this sign. I am placing a fleece of wool on the threshing floor. If there is dew only on the fleece and the ground is dry, then I will know that You will deliver Israel by my hand as You promised." In the morning, Gideon went to the threshing floor. He squeezed the fleece, and the water from it filled a bowl.

But Gideon was still afraid, so the next night he put the wool out again. This time he said to God, "I am very sorry, but I need another sign from You. In the morning let the wool be dry, but cover the ground with dew." When he woke up, the wool was dry, but dew was everywhere on the ground. Now Gideon knew for sure that God wanted him to be a leader and judge in Israel.

Gideon prepared for war against the Midianites, and he went out and gathered as many soldiers as he possibly could. Many thousand men came to be in Gideon's army. But God told Gideon the army was too big and that he would have to send back most of them. About 22,000 fighting men went home; only 10,000 remained.

But God told Gideon, "There are still too many people. Take them down to drink from the water. I will sort out which you should keep." At the water's edge, God told Gideon, "Watch how they drink. Put anyone who licks up water like a dog in one group, and those who kneel down to drink water in another group." There were 300 men who took water in their hands to lick it up like a dog. All the rest knelt down to drink. God said, "I will save Israel with the 300 men who lapped up water. I will give you a great victory over Midian. Let all the other men go home." He sent the rest of the men back to their tents. The 300 men then got their food and trumpets and followed Gideon.

God assured Gideon that they would be enough to win the battle. God had a very smart plan to defeat the large army of the Midianites with only 300 Israelite soldiers. God explained to Gideon that each soldier must carry a torch, a clay pot, and a horn. Gideon instructed his men to light their torches, but to cover them with the clay pots to hide the light. In this way, they could sneak into the Midianites camp without being discovered. Then, on Gideon's signal, every man smashed his clay pot and blew his horn.

The Midianites woke up from their sleep when they heard the loud noise of the trumpets blowing. Gideon had also put men in the hills all around the Midianite camp. When the Midianites woke up and saw light on the hilltops and the loud sound of blowing horns, it looked as if a very, very large army had surrounded them. It seemed as if there was no way to escape.

The Midianites began running out of their tents to try and get away. But in the darkness, they ran into one another and thought their enemies were already in the camp fighting them. So they started fighting one another in the darkness, and the Midianites destroyed themselves. In this way God, gave Gideon and his 300 men a great victory over a much larger army.

During the 40 years Gideon was judge, there was peace in Israel.

Samson

(Judges 13-16)

When Gideon died, God sent a new judge and leader to Israel. His name was Samson. Samson's father was named Manoah. Although he and his wife wanted to have children, they did not have any. Years passed by. But one day God's angel came and stood before her and said, "You have been unable to have children, but soon you will be pregnant and will give birth to a son. Be careful not to drink any wine or strong drink. I promise, you will have a son. You must never cut his hair. The child will be used by God to be a judge in Israel and save God's people from their enemies. Remember: From his birth until his death, he must never cut his hair as a sign that he belongs to God."

And it happened as the angel said. Manoah's wife gave birth to a son and named him Samson. God blessed Samson as he grew up.

Samson never allowed anyone to cut his hair. As a young man, Samson already proved that he was super strong. Once, he fought a big lion that attacked him, but Samson easily killed the lion with his bare hands.

The Philistines caused trouble for God's people. God helped Samson protect His people from the Philistines. One night, Samson was staying in a city called Gaza. The city was surrounded by a tall, thick wall, and it had very big gates for protection. When the Philistines found out that Samson was in the city, they wanted to catch him. So they locked the gates, trying to keep Samson trapped inside the city walls. But Samson easily tore the gates off of the wall, put them on his back, and carried them away from the city. The Philistines were shocked to see how strong Samson was.

Samson fell in love with a woman named Delilah. The Philistines used money to get Delilah to help them capture Samson. They promised her several thousand shekels of silver if she would give them the secret to his strength. At first Samson told her that if he were tied with fresh bowstrings, he would be weak. Delilah tested him with Philistine warriors ready to capture him. She cried when he was easily able to break the bowstrings. Then he said that new ropes could hold him. Again, he easily broke free. Delilah pleaded with him again, and he told her that if the seven locks of his hair were woven into a loom, he would be unable to escape. Delilah had his hair woven, making it tight with pins as he slept. But when he woke up, he easily broke free.

"God, please give me back my powers just one more time." And God made Samson strong again.

Finally Delilah said, "If you really loved me, you would tell me the secret to your strength, instead of making a fool of me." She continued to nag and beg and plead with him until he finally gave in.

He told her, "The secret to my strength is that my hair has never been cut. I have been bound by a vow to God from the time of my birth. If my head is shaved, my strength will vanish."

When Delilah saw that he had told her everything, she sent word to the rulers of the Philistines, "Come back once more. He has told me everything." So while he was sleeping, Delilah had Samson's hair cut off. Immediately, Samson's strength left him. Now the Philistines could easily catch Samson. They tied him up and threw him in prison. They were afraid Samson would escape so they blinded him by tearing out his eyes. In the prison, Samson was forced to push a big heavy stone to grind grain, but the hair on his head began to grow again after it had been shaved.

One day, the Philistines held a big party in their temple to celebrate their god Dagon. During the party they had the evil plan to make fun of Samson, so they brought him up from the prison. They shouted, "Bring out Samson to entertain us." More than 3,000 people were gathered, and many were laughing at blind Samson. He was chained between the pillars of the building with a hand on each one.

Much of Samson's hair had grown back in the prison. He prayed his last prayer, "God, please give me back my powers just one more time." And God made him strong again. Samson pushed as hard as he could, and the big pillars began to break. The roof came crashing down on everyone. Down came the temple on the rulers and all the people in it. Thus Samson killed many more when he died than while he lived. He had led Israel for 20 years.

The Boy Samuel

(1 Samuel 1-3)

Years later, Samuel became Israel's next great leader. Before Samuel was born, his mother Hannah had prayed and prayed to have children, but she did not have any. She was married to a man named Elkanah.

Years passed by, and one day Hannah made a promise to God. "If I have a son," she said, "he will be Your special servant all of his life." Eli was a priest in God's tabernacle, and he watched as Hannah prayed. He could see she was moving her mouth but no words came out so Eli thought she was drunk. "How long will you continue in your drunkenness? Get rid of your wine," Eli said.

Hannah answered, "No. I am not drunk. I am a woman who is deeply troubled. I have not had any wine or any strong drink. I have been pouring out my soul in grief, begging God to bring me out of my deep sadness." Eli then replied, "Go in peace. May the God of Israel answer your prayers."

A few months later, Hannah realized that she was going to have a baby. When her son was born, Hannah named him Samuel, saying, "I have asked the Lord for him."

Samuel sat up and said,
"Speak, Lord, for Your
servant is listening."

When Samuel was still very young, Hannah brought him back to Eli, the priest. Eli had two sons who were also priests, but they did not honor or obey God. They did not want to help their old father. Hannah said to Eli, "I want Samuel to grow up working here with you. It is a promise I had made to God before Samuel was born, and now I want to keep my promise."

Hannah visited Samuel at the tabernacle every year, and every year she brought him a new coat. Eli, the priest, loved Samuel dearly and treated him like he was his own son. Eli told Samuel all about God, and he also taught him everything about being a servant in God's tabernacle. Samuel continued to serve God even though he was just a boy helping Eli in the tabernacle. He was growing in favor with the Lord and men.

Years went by, and Samuel continued to serve the Lord. At that time, there were not many visions. God did not speak directly to anyone. Eli's eyesight was failing, and he slept in his own room. Samuel was asleep by the lamp stand in the Holy Place, near the Ark of God. One night while Samuel was sleeping in the tabernacle, he heard a voice. The voice was calling his name, "Samuel! Samuel!"

"Here I am," said Samuel, running to Eli. "Here I am. You called me."

Eli said, "I did not call you. Go back to sleep."

Samuel went back and lay down. God called again, "Samuel!"

Again Samuel ran to Eli and said, "Here I am, for you called me."

But Eli said, "I did not call you. Lie down again."

Samuel did not know God, because He had not spoken to him before. When God called Samuel a third time, Samuel again went to Eli and said, "Here I am. You called me."

Eli finally understood that it was God was calling the young man. Eli said to him, "Go and lie down. If He calls again say, 'Speak, Lord. Your servant is listening.'" So Samuel went back to the Holy Place and lay down.

God came and stood before Samuel again, calling, "Samuel, Samuel."

Samuel sat up and said, "Speak, Lord, for Your servant is listening."

From that night on, God often spoke to Samuel. People soon learned that Samuel talked with God, so more and more people came to Samuel for advice. He became a prophet while he was still just a boy because God was speaking to him about things to come. Samuel continued to grow. God was with him and made everything he said come true.

David and Goliath

(1 Samuel 8-9; 15-17; Psalm 23)

Samuel was a leader in Israel many years and taught people to follow God. He was a good man, and he loved God. But when Samuel was getting older, the Israelites demanded to have a new leader. They did not just want a leader, but they wanted to have a real king like many other nations had. So they demanded that Samuel find them someone to be king and to lead Israel. Samuel had two sons, but they were not honest or fair, so they could not be trusted. Instead, Samuel found the king God had chosen. He was an impressive young man named Saul. He was a head taller than anybody and a strong warrior. The people really expected that he would be a great king for them. They were especially hoping he could defeat their worst enemy, the Philistines. The Philistines were Israel's fiercest enemy, and over and over again they attacked Israel.

Now the Philistines had gathered their armies for battle. They were camped on the mountain on one side of the Valley of Elah, and the Israelites were camped on the other side of the valley. The leader of the Philistines was a champion by the name of Goliath, who stood over nine feet tall. He had a bronze helmet on his head and wore a coat of bronze plates that weighed about 125 pounds. He had bronze armor on his legs. A bronze javelin was slung between his shoulders. The shaft of his spear was like a weaver's beam; the head of the spear weighed about 15 pounds. His shield bearer went ahead of him.

Goliath stood and called out to the armies of Israel, "Why do you come out, lining up for battle? Am I not a Philistine, and are you not servants of Saul? Choose a man to fight me. If he can kill me, then we will be your servants. But if I am the winner, then you will be our servants. I challenge your army! Let us fight!"

When Saul and his men heard Goliath's words, they were terrified. For 40 days, the Philistine came forward and repeated his taunts every morning and evening.

Then one day a young man named David came to the camp to visit his brothers who were soldiers in the army.

"You are fighting me with your sword, spear, and all your strength. But I am fighting with the strength God will give me."

David was a shepherd who took care of the family's sheep. David could see Goliath and see how everyone was afraid of him, but David was not afraid. David went up to King Saul and said, "I am not afraid of Goliath and will fight him." But Saul said, "You are just a boy. How can you fight and defeat the giant?" David replied, "With God's help, I have killed lions and bears who tried to steal my sheep. God will also help me fight Goliath."

When Saul heard these brave words, he gave David his own sword and dressed him with the king's helmet and armor. David tried on Saul's armor. He walked around in it but gave it back to Saul. "I can't wear this. I am not used to fighting in it."

Taking his shepherd's staff, David went by a small brook and chose five smooth stones. He put them in his pouch. With his sling in his hand, David approached Goliath.

At the same time, Goliath and his shield bearer came closer to David. Goliath hated David because he was a handsome young man. "Am I a dog that you come out against me with sticks?" He prayed to his gods and cursed David. "Come on! I will give your body to the birds in the air and the beasts of the field!"

David answered him, "You are fighting me with your sword, spear, and all your strength. But I am fighting with the strength God will give me."

As the Philistine came forward, David ran quickly to meet him. Reaching into his pouch, he put a stone in his sling, hurling it at the giant. It struck Goliath in the forehead, sinking in. He fell facedown to the ground. So David defeated the Philistine with a stone and sling. There was no sword in David's hand. God had given David the strength to kill the giant, and David gave God the glory for the victory.

As King Saul saw David going out against the Philistine, he asked Abner, the captain of his army, "Abner, whose son is that?" Abner did not know. After David killed Goliath, Abner brought him before Saul. King Saul asked, "Whose son are you, young man?" David answered, "I am the son of your servant Jesse of Bethlehem."

The Philistines were shocked to see that their giant, Goliath, was defeated by a young man, and they ran away. But all the soldiers in Israel's army were excited and celebrated how David had just defeated Goliath with God's help. David became a famous hero in Israel.

Many years later when Saul died, the people made David their new king. David was a great king and built a mighty kingdom and defeated Israel's many enemies. He also captured the city of Jerusalem and built his big palace in the city. David was a good king because he followed and listened to God. David was skilled with many things. He was both a great warrior but also a wonderful poet and musician at the same time. David played the harp and wrote many songs about God's love and about trusting God with the difficulties of life.

Wise King Solomon

(1 Kings 1-3; 6-8)

David's son Solomon became king after David. One night, God appeared to Solomon in a dream and said, "What do you think I should give you?" King Solomon said, "You have showed my father, David, great mercy. Now, I pray that you will give me an understanding mind to govern these people, that I will be able to understand what is good and what is evil."

God was pleased that Solomon asked for this. He said, "Because you have asked for this, and not to live a long life, or for personal riches, or for the lives of your enemies, but have asked to understand what is good and what is evil, I will give you what you have asked. I will give you a wise and understanding heart so that there never was, nor will there ever be, anyone as wise as you. I will also give you what you have not requested: riches and honor, so that no other king on earth can compare with you for as long as you live." Solomon woke up and was very happy. He returned to Jerusalem and had a big party where all his servants had a great feast.

Many times Solomon showed how wise he was. One day two women came before King Solomon and asked him to be the judge of their problem. One woman said, "My lord, this woman and I live in the same house. I gave birth to a son while she was there. Three days later she also gave birth to a son. We were alone in the house with our babies. Then this woman's child died in the night because she lay on top of him. She awoke at midnight, took my child from beside me as I slept, and put her dead child by my side. She took my child into her own arms. When I awoke in the morning to nurse my child, I looked and saw that it was dead. Then I looked closely at the baby in the morning light and saw that it was not my son."

The other woman said, "No, the living child is mine. The dead child is yours."

The first woman kept on saying, "No, the dead child is yours. The living child is mine." They argued like this before the king.

"Give the first woman the living child. Do not kill him. She is his mother."

King Solomon then said, "This one says, 'My son is alive, and your son is dead.' The other one says, 'No! Your son is dead, and mine is the living one.' Bring me a sword!" A sword was brought before the king. The king said, "Cut the baby into two pieces. Give half of the baby to one woman and give half of the baby to the other woman."

Then the woman of the living child was filled with love as she thought of her baby boy. "Oh my lord, give her the living child. I beg you, do not kill him." But the other woman said, "He will be neither yours nor mine. Cut him in two."

The king answered, "Give the first woman the living child. Do not kill him. She is his mother."

Then all Israel heard about the judgment the king had given. They were in awe of the wisdom God had given him to be a faithful judge.

When Solomon had reigned for three years, he began to build the Temple. The Temple was beautiful! The foundation and building stones were cut on the quarry site so that no iron tool was heard as it was being built. Side rooms were made for storage. Carvings of palm trees, flowers, and angels were made in the cedar paneling of the walls and doors. The carvings and floors were covered with gold. Two cherubim were made to stand guard over the Ark of the Covenant in the Most Holy Place. Curtains separated it from the Holy Place, where priests served. The gold lamp stands and altars of incense stood in the Holy Place. Outside, in the courtyard, there was an altar for burnt sacrifices and a huge basin for washing.

Finally the beautiful Temple was finished. It had taken seven years to build. The Ark of the Covenant, which contained the stone tablets Moses had received from the Lord God, was brought up and placed inside the Most Holy Place. As the priests came out of the Holy Place, the glory of the Lord filled the entire Temple. Then Solomon offered a sacrifice of 22,000 cattle and 120,000 sheep. For fourteen days, the people of Israel celebrated at the dedication of the Temple, rejoicing for all the good things God had done for the people of Israel.

Elijah—Fire from Heaven

(1 Kings 16-18)

After King Solomon, there were many very bad kings in Israel who did not care about God at all. Instead, they built all kinds of idols made of rock and wood. One of the worst kings was Ahab. He decided that everybody should worship a god named Baal. Almost everyone obeyed the king, because King Ahab had declared that anyone who worshipped the God of the Israelites would be killed.

But seven thousand people in Israel still believed in the true God, and one of them was a prophet named Elijah. God told Elijah to go and tell King Ahab that God would not let rain fall in Israel for a very long time. For the next few years, it would not rain, and there would not be any dew. This was punishment because Ahab was teaching the people to worship Baal. When the rain stopped, the plants and crops did not grow. It was very difficult to find anything to eat.

But Elijah was safe, far away from King Ahab. God told him where to go where He would take care of him. Even though everything in the land was now completely dried out because no rain had fallen for months, Elijah was living well by a little stream that still had water. Every morning large birds brought pieces of bread and meat to Elijah. He had more than enough food to eat every day. In this way, God kept Elijah alive with help of the birds He sent for as long as Elijah had to hide from the evil king's soldiers.

Three years went by, but King Ahab continued to be a stubborn and evil person who did not want to follow God. Instead he built more and more idols to Baal. God sent Elijah to the king and said, "Why do you still worship Baal?

"Lord, God of Abraham, Isaac, and Jacob, make it known this day that You are God."

"Let us now have a contest between the true Living God and your Baal who is no god at all. This will prove for good which God is real."

King Ahab agreed to the contest and gathered all the leaders of Israel on a high mountain. The king also brought hundreds of priests who believed in Baal. Then they would build two altars: one for God and one for Baal. The priests of Baal built an altar and put wood on it. Then the priests of Baal cut up a bull to offer as a sacrifice to Baal. Elijah said, "Don't set the wood on fire. Instead you can pray to your god Baal. If he is real, he can light the fire on the altar. I will pray to the Living God. Let us then agree that from this day on we will believe in the God who sends fire from the heavens."

Hundreds of priests begged Baal to light a fire on the altar. But nothing at all happened. Elijah began to taunt them. "Shout louder!" he said. "Surely he is a god! Perhaps he is deep in thought, or busy, or traveling. Maybe he is sleeping and must be awakened." But still, nothing happened. Baal was not God but just a piece of rock, wood, and imagination.

They cried louder, cutting themselves with knives until the blood gushed, as was their custom. They danced and cried aloud all afternoon, but no one spoke or answered or paid any attention to them at all.

Then it was Elijah's turn. He repaired the altar of the Lord using twelve large stones, one stone for each of the families of Israel. Then Elijah dug a large trench all around the altar. He put the wood and the bull on the altar. Surprisingly, Elijah commanded that four big jars of water should be poured out all over the altar. Elijah told them to pour the jars of water over the altar two more times so that twelve jars of water had been poured on the altar. The bull, the wood, and stones were very wet, and there was water in the trench around the altar. Everybody watched closely as Elijah raised his hands and quietly prayed to God.

Elijah stepped forward and said, "Lord, God of Abraham, Isaac, and Jacob, make it known this day that You are God in Israel and that I am Your servant who has done this by Your command. Answer me, God, so that these people may know that You are the true God of Israel."

After he had prayed a huge flame suddenly came down from the sky and hit the altar. The flame from the sky burned up everything on the altar. Even the big stone altar burned up, and the water around the altar disappeared as well. The people were amazed! They all fell on their knees and shouted, "God is the true God! God is the true God!"

"Arrest the prophets of Baal," Elijah said. "Do not let them escape." Then God sent rain to His people again.

Jonah and the Fish

(Jonah 1-3)

There was a man named Jonah, and there was a city called Nineveh. Back then Nineveh was one of the biggest cities in the world, but also one of the most terrible ones because people there were evil and did terrible things to one another. This made God very angry, and He said, "Jonah, go to Nineveh, to that great city. Tell them that I have seen their wickedness." Jonah did not want to go to Nineveh. The people of Nineveh were enemies of God's people, and Jonah did not want to give them God's message. So, instead he went down to the harbor at Joppa and bought a ticket to sail to Tarshish. He thought that he could run away from God by taking a ship sailing in the opposite direction.

Jonah went down below deck to try and get some sleep. He wanted to try and forget that he actually was escaping from the job God had asked him to do. But God sent a great wind upon the sea. So mighty was the storm that they thought the ship would break apart. The sailors were very afraid, and each one prayed to his own gods, begging them to stop the storm. When that did not stop the storm, they threw the ship's cargo into the sea to make the load lighter.

As the storm continued, the captain discovered that Jonah was sleeping soundly down in the lowest part of the ship. The captain shouted at Jonah, "How can you sleep at a time like this? Get up and call on your God. Maybe He will have mercy on us so that we won't die in this storm."

The sailors said to one another, "Let's cast lots to see who is causing the storm." Each sailor took his turn, and the lot fell on Jonah. The sailors said, "Tell us why this is happening to us. What is your job? What is your country? Who are your people?"

"A big fish came and swallowed
Jonah in one mouthful."

He answered them, "I am an Israelite. I worship the Lord God, who made the heavens and the seas and the dry land."

The sailors were terrified. They asked him, "What did you do to make God so angry?" He told them that he was trying to run away from God.

"What can we do so that God will stop the storm? What can we do to make your God happy?" they asked him. The seas grew wilder and wilder as the storm raged.

"Throw me over the side of the ship, and the sea will grow quiet again," Jonah answered.

This made the sailors more terrified. They tried to row the ship to shore. The storm became more furious. They could not control the ship. Finally they prayed, "Please, God, do not hold us guilty for this man's life. Do not let us die, for You have done as You wished." The sailors then picked up Jonah and threw him over the side of the ship. Immediately the storm stopped!

The crew of the ship showed that they now believed in the true God. They made a sacrifice and prayed. They made vows to serve God only.

Jonah was sinking under the water. He went deeper and deeper and deeper into the sea. He saw a big shadow approaching right under him from the depths of the sea. It came closer and closer. It was a big fish that came and swallowed Jonah alive. It swallowed him in one mouthful. Jonah went all the way down to the belly of the enormous creature. Though it was a scary, dark place to be inside the belly of the fish deep down below the sea, Jonah knew that God could still hear him. So he started to pray to God. Jonah prayed for three days and nights.

God had not forgotten Jonah. On the third day, God told the fish to spit Jonah up on the seashore.

Again God spoke to Jonah: "Get up and go to Nineveh, that great city. Tell them the message that I give you." Jonah got up and made the long journey to Nineveh. It was hundreds of miles away, but Jonah listened to what God said. Nineveh was a huge city. It took three days to walk from one end to the other. On the very first day, Jonah stood up before the people in the city and said, "In forty days, this city will be destroyed!"

The people of Nineveh listened to Jonah. They believed his message. In order to show that they were sorry for the evil they had done, they refused to eat any food. They put on rough clothing and rags. Everyone did this, from the most important people to the servants.

The king of Nineveh heard Jonah's message from God. He got up from his throne and took off his royal robes. He also put on rough clothing and rags. The king sat in a pile of ashes to show that he was sorry for the evil things that he had done as the king of Nineveh. He made a royal decree to be written and read throughout the great city. It read, "By order of the king, no one, neither man nor animal, is allowed to taste or eat anything. No one is allowed to drink anything, not even water. Everyone, even the animals, must be covered with rough clothing. Everyone must cry to God the Lord. The people must repent of their evil ways and the violence they have done. Who knows, maybe God will change His mind. Maybe He will turn from His anger so that we do not die!"

When God saw what they had done, that they were truly sorry for their evil ways, He changed His mind. He did not destroy the city as He had planned to do. God showed His great love to Jonah by rescuing him from the sea. He gave him the opportunity to share God's love with a huge city. God wanted everyone who lived there to become His children.

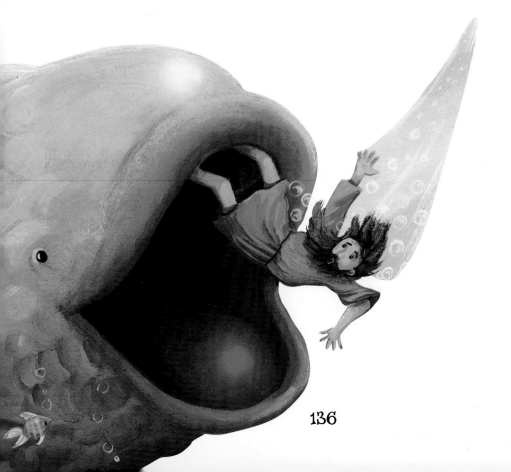

The Fiery Furnace

(Daniel 1-3)

For many years, God's people refused to follow His commands. Because of this, God allowed Nebuchadnezzar, King of Babylon, to conquer the city of Jerusalem. Nebuchadnezzar ordered that the young men of Israel from the royal family be brought to Babylon. The boys were to be handsome, intelligent, and able to learn the language and customs of the Babylonians.

Among them were four young men who trusted in God. Their names were Daniel, Shadrach, Meshach, and Abednego. They were put in King Nebuchadnezzar's house to work for him. Nebuchadnezzar was one of the most powerful kings Babylon ever had and was also a very evil person. One day King Nebuchadnezzar built a huge idol that was 90 feet tall and nine feet wide. King Nebuchadnezzar did not know or care about God. So, instead he had the idol covered with gold and placed it where everyone could see it.

Then a message was sent out to the whole city, "All peoples and nations, when you hear the sound of the cornet, flute, harp, bagpipe, lute, lyre, and all the music, all of you must bow down and worship the King Nebuchadnezzar's wonderful golden statue. If you do not bow down and worship the golden statue, you will be thrown into a burning, fiery furnace." So when all the people heard the sound of the cornet, flute, harp, bagpipe, lute, lyre, and all the music, they all bowed down and worshipped the huge image.

But some of the king's servants brought some surprising news. "O king, may you live forever! You have decreed that when all the people and nations hear the sound of the cornet, flute, harp, bagpipe, lute, lyre, and all the music, they must bow down and worship the wonderful image you have set up, and if they do not bow down, they must be thrown into a burning, fiery furnace. Did you know, king, that there are some Jews from the land of Israel that work for you—Shadrach, Meshach, and Abednego—who do not worship our gods? They will not bow down to the image."

The king was furious and sent for them. "Is it true, Shadrach, Meshach, and Abednego, that you will not bow down and worship the statue? Now I will give you another chance. When you hear the music

of the cornet, flute, harp, bagpipe, lute, lyre, and all the music, and you bow down, it will be good. If you do not bow down, I must have you thrown immediately into the burning, fiery furnace."

But Shadrach, Meshach, and Abednego said to him, "O Nebuchadnezzar, we don't have to worry about answering you. If our God is willing to save us, He will save us, because He has the power to rescue us from the burning, fiery furnace. But even if He should choose not to save us, we will not worship your gods or the idol that you have put up."

King Nebuchadnezzar was so furious that his face twisted with rage. He ordered the furnace to be heated seven times hotter than usual. He had very strong soldiers tie up Shadrach, Meshach, and Abednego, still dressed in their official cloaks, their turbans, and tunics.

"I put three people in the fire. But now I see four men in the furnace, and one of them looks like the Son of God."

The soldiers threw the men headfirst into the burning, fiery furnace. Because the furnace was so extremely hot, the soldiers that tied the three men were killed by the heat from the fire.

But then an amazing thing happened. The fire did not hurt the three friends. It did not even burn their clothes, and they began walking around inside the furnace. But now there were four people inside the furnace. The king was horrified when he saw this and said, "I put three people in the fire. But now I see four men in the furnace, and one of them looks like the Son of God."

The king went to the furnace and called, "Shadrach, Meshach, and Abednego, servants of the Most High God, come out of the fire." Calmly, the three friends walked out of the furnace. They did not even smell burnt from the fires they had been in. King Nebuchadnezzar knew that God had saved them and realized how strong God is. Therefore, the king decided to send out a new law in the vast country of Babylon demanding that no one must ever say anything bad about the God of Israel. Daniel's friends had trusted in God, and He had saved them. Now everybody came to know what God had done on this day all over Babylon. Then the king promoted Shadrach, Meshach, and Abednego to higher positions in the kingdom.

Daniel and the Lions

(Daniel 6)

Daniel was wise and honest in everything he did. God was with Daniel, and the kings gave him important work in their kingdoms in Babylon. The kings liked Daniel very much, especially King Darius. But some of the other leaders in the palace did not like Daniel because they were jealous that the kings trusted him with so much. They decided to set up a trap for Daniel. They knew Daniel prayed to God three times every day, so they went to the king and said, "Why don't you make a new law that for the next thirty days, people can only pray to you? Then people can show they are only loyal to you as their king. If they pray to anyone else, they will be thrown into the lions' den." The king liked this idea and made this a law that could not be changed.

When Daniel learned that the king had signed the law, he went to his upstairs room. He opened his windows that faced Jerusalem. He continued to kneel down to say prayers of praise and thanksgiving three times a day, just as he had always done.

The men rushed in and found Daniel on his knees in prayer asking God to help him. They rushed to the king and reminded him of his decision: "Didn't you publish a decree that says for the next 30 days if anyone prays to any god or man, except to you, king, that he would be thrown into a den of lions?"

King Darius said, "Yes, that law stands in accordance with the laws of the Medes and the Persians. It cannot be changed or cancelled."

Then they said, "King Darius, Daniel, who is one of the men we took from Israel, does not show respect for you or the laws that you have published. He still prays to his God three times a day."

The king was very, very sad when he heard this because he liked Daniel so much. But at the same time, he also knew that, being the king, he had to enforce the law. He tried to think of a way to rescue Daniel all day, but was unsuccessful. The governors and prime ministers came to Darius and said, "Remember, that according to the laws no decisions made by the king can be changed."

So, the king gave orders for Daniel to be brought to the lions' den. Daniel was thrown into the pit by the king's soldiers. King Darius said, "May your God, whom you continually worship, rescue you." A stone was put over the entrance of the pit. The king sealed it with his signet ring. The governors and prime ministers also sealed it with their signet rings so that nothing would be changed, as ordered.

During the night the king could not sleep, and he stayed awake all night in his palace. He did not drink or eat anything, and he was thinking all the time about the terrible lions and poor Daniel.

Early in the morning, as soon as the first sunlight came up, the king rushed out to the lions' den. Even though he did not expect an answer he called, "Daniel! Daniel! Are you there?"

Daniel answered, "O king, may you live forever! My God sent His angel to shut the mouths of the lions. They have not harmed me. God has kept me safe from the lions."

The king rejoiced and gave orders for Daniel to be lifted from the lions' den. As he examined Daniel, the king saw that there were no scratches or wounds on him, because he had trusted in God. The king commanded that the men who had falsely accused Daniel be thrown into the lions' den instead.

Then King Darius wrote to every people, in every language throughout the entire kingdom of Babylon, "Peace to all of you! I issue a decree that in every land of my kingdom, men must fear and tremble before the God of Daniel. He is the living God and will live forever. His kingdom will never be destroyed. He will rule until the end of time. He rescues and delivers; He works signs and wonders in heaven and on earth. He has rescued Daniel from the power of the lions."

Daniel continued to prosper during the entire reign of King Darius.

Queen Esther

(Book of Esther)

King Xerxes of Persia needed a wife. His servants searched from India to Ethiopia to find the most beautiful women in the land. Many young women were brought to the palace including a beautiful young Israelite woman named Esther. When King Xerxes saw Esther, he was very pleased! He was so pleased, he set the royal crown on her head and Esther became the queen. To celebrate the king held a big party for all his nobles and officials. Esther's banquet lasted 180 days.

Esther's cousin Mordecai had adopted Esther as a child. Mordecai was also an Israelite or Jew, but the king did not know anything about Esther's family background when she became his queen. One day when Mordecai went out and sat by the palace gates, he overheard some men planning to kill the king. He immediately went to Esther and

warned her so she could tell this to the king. The bad men were then arrested, and the king was very grateful to Mordecai for his help. The story of Mordecai's rescue of the king was written in the royal books.

After this, an advisor named Haman was placed in honor above all the leaders in the kingdom. The king commanded everyone to bow to Haman, but Mordecai refused. The king's officials asked Mordecai each day why he would not bow down to honor Haman. "I am a Jew," Mordecai said. When Mordecai would not bow to honor him, Haman was furious. Haman made plans to destroy all the Jews in the entire kingdom of Xerxes.

Haman cast lots to choose a good day for this to happen. Then he went to King Xerxes and said, "There are a certain people throughout your kingdom with laws different from your laws. It is not in your interest to allow them to live in your kingdom. Let it be decided that they must all be killed."

The king took his ring and sealed the decree so that it would surely happen. The decision was written in every language and sent to all people. It gave permission to destroy, kill, and annihilate all Jews—young and old, men, women, and children—on the thirteenth day of the twelfth month. All of the Israelites in Babylon would die.

Mordecai tore his clothes and put ashes on his head when he discovered Haman's plot. Jews everywhere also fasted and wept. Esther called for Mordecai to come to see her. She sent clothing so that he could enter the palace. Mordecai refused to come to Esther. He sent her the letter of Haman's plot and urged her to go to the king to save her people.

Esther sent a message to Mordecai, "All the people of the kingdom know that if a man or woman goes to the king in the inner court without being called, they will be put to death—unless the king holds out to them the golden scepter. Then they will live."

Mordecai sent this message back to Esther: "Do not think that because you live in the palace you will be saved. If you do not speak up, we will be killed. Who knows? Maybe this is why you have come to the kingdom." Esther replied, "Go and gather the Jews. Have them fast and pray for me. My servant girls and I will also fast and pray. Then I will go to the king, even though it is against the law. If I die, then I die."

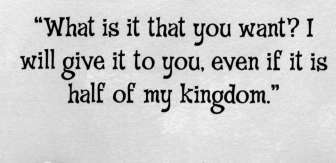

"What is it that you want? I
will give it to you, even if it is
half of my kingdom."

Esther put on her royal gown and went to the king as he sat on the throne. When King Xerxes saw her standing there, he was pleased, and he held out the golden scepter to her. "What is it you ask, Queen Esther? I will give you anything, up to half of my kingdom," Xerxes said.

Esther asked, "If it pleases the king, let him come with Haman to a banquet that I have prepared."

The king and Haman quickly went to the feast. As they were eating and drinking, the king asked again, "What is it that you want? I will give it to you, even if it is half of my kingdom."

Esther replied, "If I have found favor with you, my king, come again to dine with me tomorrow with Haman. I will tell you then what I request."

The next day once again, in the middle of the feast, the King asked Esther, "What do you wish, Queen Esther? I will grant it, up to half my kingdom."

Queen Esther said, "If I have found favor in your sight, my king, let my life be spared. Please save the lives of my people. My people and I have been sold to be destroyed and killed."

"Who has done this? Where can I find him? Who is planning to do this evil?" shouted King Xerxes.

Esther pointed at Haman and said, "This wicked man is our enemy."

Now, the king got very angry. He realized how Haman had convinced him to make such a wrong decision. So, instead the king ordered Haman to be hung, and Mordecai was given the position of the adviser of the king. Mordecai had the king sign a new law that gave the Jewish people the right to fight back. In this way Esther was able to save herself, Mordecai, and all of the Israelite people. For this act, Esther became a very famous and respected person in Israel. Days of feasting and celebrating were held to celebrate the day when God protected His people.

Introduction to the New Testament

This section contains stories from the part of the Bible called the New Testament. It begins with the birth of God's Son, Jesus, the Savior that God had first promised to Adam and Eve. Jesus became a real man to rescue us from sin, death, and the power of the devil. These are the true events that prove that Jesus is the Savior of the whole world.

Jesus' teachings and miracles prove that He is not only from God, but together with the Holy Spirit is equal with God the Father. The Jewish leaders were jealous and made plans to kill Jesus. They became very angry as God's children began to follow Him. Their evil intentions made it appear that the devil had defeated Him.

Although Jesus had the power to save Himself, He willingly gave His life as a sacrifice for the sins of all people. This was God's plan from the very beginning. God accepted Jesus' sacrifice as He raised Him from death on the first Easter. Now we all can have forgiveness of our sins and eternal life through faith in Jesus.

May God richly bless you as you learn about Jesus, your dear Savior and Brother!

The Birth of Jesus
(Luke 1-2; Matthew 1)

A little over two thousand years ago, there was a young woman named Mary. God used her in a very special way. She lived in a small village called Nazareth, and she was planning to marry a man named Joseph. One day when Mary was at home, God's angel Gabriel suddenly stood before her and said, "Greetings, one loved by the Lord! God is with you." Mary was confused. She did not know why the angel would visit her.

Gabriel said, "Do not be afraid, Mary. God has chosen you to be the mother of His Son. You will name Him Jesus. He will be called the Son of the Most High."

Mary asked the angel, "How will this happen? I am not married, so how can I have a baby?"

The angel answered, "The Holy Spirit will come upon you. And your son will be called the Holy Son of God. Nothing is impossible for God, Mary." Mary replied, "I am the Lord's servant. Let it happen to me as you have said." Then the angel left her.

Mary was happy that she was going to be the mother of the Savior God had promised. She also wondered what Joseph would think of all this. Would he believe what the angel had said? But God took care of everything. Joseph had a dream in which an angel spoke to him, "Don't be afraid to take Mary to be your wife. This baby is God's Son. You will name Him Jesus because He will save His people from their sins." Then Joseph did as the angel said. He married Mary and brought her into his home.

About that time Caesar Augustus, the emperor, decided to have everyone registered and counted. He did this to find out how many people lived in his kingdom so he would be able to collect taxes from them. Everyone had to return to the town of his ancestors. So, Joseph went up from Nazareth to the town of Bethlehem, because he was from King David's family. Joseph and Mary had to make the long journey when it was almost time for the baby to be born.

When they arrived, Bethlehem was already crowded with others that had come to register. There was no room for them in the inn. Instead, Mary and Joseph found a place to rest where people kept their animals. Mary gave birth to Jesus, wrapped Him in soft cloths, and laid Him in a manger. God's own Son had been born, not in a fancy palace but in a dark stable.

In that same area, there were shepherds in the fields that night, taking care of their sheep. Suddenly an angel stood next to them, surrounding them with the light of God's glory. They were terrified. The angel said to them, "Don't be afraid! I bring you great news that is for all people. On this very day, in the city of David, a Savior has been born for you! He is Christ, the Lord! Look for this sign: a baby wrapped in cloths and lying in a manger." All at once, the shepherds saw an entire host

of angels all praising God and saying, "Glory to God in the highest! May God give peace on earth to men with whom He is pleased!"

When the angels left, the shepherds said to each other, "Let's go to Bethlehem and see this wonderful thing that God has told us!" They hurried to the village and found Mary and Joseph, and the baby lying in the manger. When they had seen the baby, they told others about the wonderful visit of the angels and what they said about the child. Everyone was amazed by what the shepherds told them. Mary remembered all these things and treasured them in her heart.

The shepherds returned to their fields, praising God and giving Him glory because all they had seen was exactly as the angels had told them.

Jesus Grows with God's Favor

(Luke 2; Matthew 2)

Mary and Joseph brought Jesus to the Temple in Jerusalem when He was forty days old. According to the laws given to Moses, a gift and sacrifice must be made when children were born. Usually a lamb and a dove were brought as gifts to God; however, if the family was poor, two doves could be brought. As Mary and Joseph brought the doves and little Jesus, a man named Simeon was led by the Holy Spirit to come into the Temple. He was a righteous man who loved God. Simeon took baby Jesus into his arms and praised God, saying, "Lord, now Your servant can die in peace. My eyes have seen the salvation that You have made for all people. He is a light to bring Your promises to the whole world."

Also in the Temple that day was a prophetess named Anna. She had lived at the Temple for many, many years, praying and fasting day and night. She gave thanks to God for allowing her to see baby Jesus. Anna also knew He was the Savior that God had promised to send to the world long ago.

When Jesus was born, some wise men from a country far to the east saw a magnificent star that suddenly appeared. They knew this star marked the birth of a new King among God's people, the Jews. They journeyed for hundreds of miles to Jerusalem and entered into the palace of King Herod. The wise men said, "Where is the child who was born to be the King of the Jews? We have followed the star that rose when He was born, and we have come to worship Him."

But the evil King Herod answered them, "I don't know where this new King is." He asked the people to search God's Holy Word, and they said, "God's Word says that He will be born in Bethlehem in Judea. 'Bethlehem, you will also be an important town in Judea because from you will come a Leader that will be the Shepherd of My people.'"

King Herod asked the wise men when the star first appeared. Then he told the wise men to look in Bethlehem for the new King.

Herod said, "When you find Him, let me know so I can also go and honor this new King." But Herod was lying. He wanted to kill this baby because he was jealous of anyone else who was called king in his country.

The wise men left Herod, and the star led them to the house where Jesus was. When they saw the baby and Mary, His mother, they bowed down and worshipped Him. They opened their gifts of gold, frankincense, and myrrh.

Later God warned the wise men in a dream not to go back to Herod. They left for their own country by another route. After the wise men had departed, Joseph was also warned by an angel of God in a dream. The angel said, "Joseph, get up, take the child and Mary and go quickly to Egypt. You will be safe from Herod there." That very night Joseph took Mary and Jesus and went to Egypt. They stayed in Egypt until Herod was dead. Then they returned with Jesus to their hometown of Nazareth.

"Why were you looking for Me? Did you not know that I belong here in My Father's house?"

Joseph was a skilled carpenter in Nazareth. As Jesus grew, He helped Joseph in the carpenter shop, and He also studied at the synagogue with the other boys in his village. Jesus grew, gaining wisdom and strength. God's love and blessings were upon Him.

Every year, Joseph and Mary traveled to Jerusalem to celebrate the Passover Feast. God had told Moses that His people must gather every year to remember how God rescued the Israelites from slavery in Egypt. God sent ten plagues to the Egyptians to show His power and to make Pharaoh let God's people leave. The night before the Israelites left Egypt, they painted the tops and sides of their door frames with lamb's blood. In the tenth plague, the sons of all in Egypt were killed that night, but God's angel "passed over" the blood around the doors and kept the Israelites safe. To celebrate every year, the Jews went up to the beautiful temple in Jerusalem. Many people filled the streets, and they were singing songs about what God had done for them. What a wonderful journey up to Jerusalem it was!

When Jesus was twelve years old, Joseph took his family, just as they had done in the years before. The journey to Jerusalem was more than 70 miles. They spent the week with family and friends who also went to Jerusalem for the Passover celebration. When it was time to make the long journey home, Mary and Joseph started out for Nazareth. Jesus stayed in the city, but His parents didn't know it. They thought Jesus was traveling ahead of them with some of their friends. But when they did not catch up with Him further down the road, they were worried and started looking for Him. They did not find Him, so Mary and Joseph went back to Jerusalem to search for Jesus there.

On the third day they found Him. Jesus was sitting in the temple with the teachers, listening to them and asking them questions. Everyone who listened to Jesus was amazed that His answers showed great understanding. It was very clear to them that Jesus could explain many things about God and God's Holy Word even though He was just twelve years old.

When Mary and Joseph saw Him, they were surprised. Mary said, "Son, why have you treated us like this! Your father and I have been anxiously searching for You!" But Jesus said, "Why were you looking for Me? Did you not know that I belong here in My Father's house?" Jesus said this because He knew God was His real Father.

Mary and Joseph didn't fully understand what Jesus meant, but Mary kept all these things in her heart. Jesus then left Jerusalem together with Mary and Joseph, and He stayed and grew up in Nazareth, obeying them in all things. He continued to grow wiser and taller and gained the approval of God and men.

Jesus' Baptism
(Matthew 3; Mark 1; 3-4; John 1)

There was a man who lived far from town near the Jordan River. They called him John the Baptist or John the Baptizer. He was Jesus' cousin. He spoke with powerful words and told people to be sorry for the wrong things they were doing and to stop sinning. His clothes were made from camel hair, and he wore a wide leather belt. He caught locusts and ate them with honey.

"Turn to God and be baptized," John said, "because God is about to do something wonderful very soon. Get ready. God's Messenger will soon be here." People asked John, "Are you the One who is going to save us as it is promised to us in the Bible? Are you the Messiah?" John said,

"No, I am not, but I am preparing everything for Him." So John baptized many people in the Jordan River. The people said that they were sorry for their sins and wanted to stop doing evil. They wanted to live a fresh life and follow God. When John baptized them, the people knew that God had forgiven them of their sins. People came from far away to hear his message. They confessed their sins to John, and he baptized them in the river.

One day Jesus came out to the Jordan River where John was baptizing. Jesus went over to John and asked to be baptized by him. But John said, "Jesus, You don't need to be baptized. I need to be baptized by You." John knew that Jesus was God's own Son. But Jesus insisted, "I want you to baptize Me. This is how it must be." So John baptized Jesus. When Jesus came up from the water, something wonderful happened. It was as if a gate right into heaven opened wide. A white dove came down from heaven and landed on Jesus. This was actually the Holy Spirit, who took the shape of a dove. Then the people heard the voice of God the Father, high in the sky.

God the Father said, "This is My Son. I love Him very much."

Then John told everyone, "This is God's great Messenger. This is the One I have been telling you about."

After He was baptized, Jesus went out into a desert place to be alone and to pray to God. Jesus prayed and did not eat anything for 40 days. Then the devil came to tempt Jesus, but Jesus was able to use God's Holy Word to make the devil leave Him. Jesus knew He needed God the Father and the Holy Spirit to give Him strength to do His important work on earth.

John told everyone,
"This is God's great
Messenger. This is the
One I have been telling
you about."

Jesus Calls the First Disciples
(Mark 1:16-20; 3:16-19; John 1)

Jesus was walking near where John was baptizing. John said, "Look! Here is the Lamb of God!" Two of John's disciples heard him and followed Jesus. When Jesus noticed the men following Him, He turned around and said, "What do you want?" They said, "Rabbi (which means teacher), where are You staying?"

"Come with Me and see," Jesus answered. So they went and stayed with Him all day. It was about ten o'clock in the morning when they met Him. One of the two men was Andrew, the brother of Simon Peter. Andrew came first to his brother and said, "We have found the Messiah" (which means Christ). He brought him to Jesus. Jesus said to Simon, "You are Simon, son of John. You will be called 'Cephas.'" (Cephas means rock, which in Greek is "Peter.")

Jesus was preaching to people about God and His Kingdom. Jesus lived near a large lake called the Sea of Galilee. One day as He came walking by the shore of the lake, He saw some fishing boats and some men in them. The fishermen had big nets and used them to catch fish.

Jesus called on them and said, "Come and follow Me, and I will teach you how to fish for men." Immediately, the men left their boats and nets and followed Jesus. Now Jesus already had four friends. They were called disciples, because in a special way they followed Jesus. The disciples learned from Him so they could later teach His message to others.

Soon after, Jesus met other men, and He also called them to follow Him. In all, Jesus called twelve men to be His disciples: Simon, also called Peter, James and John, Andrew, Philip, Bartholomew, Matthew, Thomas, James the son of Alphaeus, Thaddaeus, Simon the Zealot, and Judas who later betrayed Him. During the next three years, these twelve men followed Jesus everywhere as they traveled to many places in Israel.

"Come and follow Me,
and I will teach you how
to fish for men."

Jesus Turns Water into Wine

(John 2)

Jesus and some of His disciples were invited to a big wedding in Cana. Jesus' mother, Mary, was also invited. There were many friends and relatives celebrating. They served the most wonderful food and wine. Beautiful music was played as the people sang and danced. Everybody was happy and celebrated with the young couple that had just been married. But during the party, Mary came to Jesus and brought some bad news, "I have found out that the wine is all gone, and they don't have more to serve. Can you help them?"

Mary then said to the servants, "Do whatever He tells you to do." There were six large stone jars. Each jar usually held about twenty to thirty gallons of water.

Jesus told the servants, "Fill the jars with water." The servants filled them to the very top. Then Jesus said, "Take some out and give it to the man in charge of the feast." So they took it to him.

The manager of the feast took a drink. It wasn't water anymore! Jesus used His power to make the water change into wine. The manager did not know where the wine was from, but the servants who had filled the jars with water and dipped the wine out of the jars knew. The manager called to the groom and said, "Everyone serves the best wine first, and then, when the people have had enough to drink, they serve the wine that is not as good. However, you have saved the best for now!"

God had given Jesus the power to change water into wine. It was not a magic trick. It was a miracle. A miracle is a special sign where God shows His power. This was

The manager of the
feast took a drink.
It wasn't water anymore!
Jesus used His power
to make the water
change into wine.

182

only the first of many miracles Jesus did. In His life, Jesus did many more miracles to show that He was the Son of God. He showed His glory, and His disciples were filled with joy and amazement.

Soon after that, Jesus went to Jerusalem to celebrate the Passover. In the temple He found people selling oxen, sheep, and doves. Jesus made a whip of cords and drove the sheep and oxen out of the temple area. He scattered the coins as He turned over the tables. When He saw people selling doves, He said, "Take these away! How dare you turn My Father's house into a market!"

The Jews demanded, "What sign will You do to show us that You have the right to do these things?"

Jesus answered, "Destroy this temple, and in three days, I will raise it up."

The Jewish leaders said, "It has taken 46 years to build this temple. You are going to build it again in three days?" But Jesus was speaking about His body. After He had risen from the dead, His disciples remembered what He had said. They believed the Scripture and the words Jesus had said.

Jesus Teaches about the Sower

(Mark 4; Matthew 13; Luke 8)

Again Jesus began to teach the people by the side of the sea. The crowd was so large that He got into a boat and put it out from the shore. The multitude of people listened from the shore. Jesus spoke to them in many parables. (A parable is a short story about things on earth that explains truths about heaven and tells what God is like.)

Jesus told a very interesting story about a farmer who was planting his crop. With his big basket of seed for grain, he went out in the field and tossed the seed here and there, all over his field. This is how the farmers planted long ago in Israel.

Jesus said, "As the farmer sowed it, some of the seed landed on the path. The birds came and ate it up. Some of the seed fell where the ground was rocky. It did not have much soil to grow. Immediately it sprang up, because the soil was shallow. When the sun came up, it burned up the plants. They withered away because they did not have deep roots. Other seed fell among the thorns. When the thorns grew up and choked the plants, they did not produce a crop."

"The soil on the path, the soil filled with stones, the soil filled with weeds and thorns, and the good soil, are like four different kinds of people and how they listen to My words, the seeds."

Then Jesus said, "But some seed fell on the good soil. It grew up and produced a crop, with thirty, sixty, or a hundred times as much grain as was planted."

Later, when Jesus was alone with the twelve disciples and some others, they asked Jesus about the story. Jesus answered, "This story is really about how people listen to what I have to say. The seeds are God's Word. The soil on the path, the soil filled with stones, the soil filled with weeds and thorns, and the good soil, are like four different kinds of people and how they listen to My words, the seeds.

"The first kind of people don't listen at all because their hearts are hard like the ground along the path. The devil comes and takes God's Word away so they won't believe.

"The second kind of people listen to God's Word gladly at first, but then quickly again lose interest. They are like the soil filled with stones. Because their faith is not strong, like plants without good roots, they get worried and fall into temptation. They do not grow, but dry up like a plant in the hot sun.

"The third kind of people is like the soil with weeds and thorns. They grow tall and healthy at first, but their desire for riches and the pleasures of life choke out God's Word, like weeds and thorns tangle up with good plants and kill them. They are so distracted by what money can buy that their love for God dies.

"Finally, the fourth kind of people is those who in their hearts are like the good soil in the story. They listen to what I teach them about God. Therefore God's love grows in their hearts every day just

188

like a strong plant that grows a little day by day. These people will surely become filled with true joy because they follow and live by My words. Their faith will grow and produce many more seeds of God's Word to be planted again and again."

The Stilling of the Storm

(Luke 8:22-56)

Jesus had been teaching people all day about God and His love for us. Jesus said to His disciples, "Let's cross to the other side of the lake." They left the crowd on the shore and got ready to sail across the Sea of Galilee. Jesus was tired. As they sailed, He fell asleep in the back of the boat. Without warning, a terrible storm came upon the sea. The wind caused great waves to wash over the side of the boat so that it filled with water. Jesus went on sleeping. Although some of the disciples were fishermen who spent their days working on this sea, they were terrified. They went to Jesus and woke Him, saying, "Master, we are drowning!"

Jesus got up. He said to the disciples, "Why are you afraid? Your faith is so weak." He harshly scolded the wind, "Hush!" He said to the sea, "Peace. Be still!" Immediately the wind stopped blowing, and it was completely calm.

The disciples were filled with great fear, but were amazed saying, "Who is this? He commands the wind and the sea, and they obey Him!"

A crowd gathered to welcome Jesus when He returned from the boat. Jairus, a leader of the local synagogue, knelt at Jesus' feet. He pleaded with Jesus, "My little girl is dying. Please come and lay Your hand on her so that she will live."

This was his only daughter, a girl who was twelve years old.

As Jesus made His way to Jairus's house, a messenger came and said, "Jairus! Your daughter is dead. Do not bother Jesus to come anymore." When Jesus heard this, He said to Jairus, "Do not be afraid. Just believe, and she will be healed."

Jesus continued to the house with Peter, James, and John. When they arrived, there was a large crowd of people crying loudly. Sad songs were played on flutes. Jesus said to the people mourning, "Do not cry. The child is not dead. She is sleeping."

But the mourners laughed at Jesus. They could see that she was really dead.

Jesus went straight into the room where the dead child lay. He took Peter, James, John, and the girl's parents with Him. Jesus went over and took the girl by the hand and said, "Talitha koum," which means in Aramaic, "Little girl, I say to you, arise." Immediately the girl got up and began to walk around. The parents were overcome with amazement! He told them to give her something to eat. Jesus strictly told them that they should not tell anyone about this, but soon a message went out to the whole land about what wonderful miracles Jesus had done, even making a dead girl come alive again.

Jesus Feeds Thousands

(Matthew 14; Mark 6; Luke 9; John 6)

Jesus got into a boat and crossed the Sea of Galilee. Jesus said to the disciples, "Come with Me, away from where people live, so we can rest." However, many people were looking for Jesus as He was coming to their towns. Everywhere He went huge crowds of people were following Jesus and the disciples. Many other people in the towns along the way continued to join them. They brought those who were sick, hoping that Jesus would heal them. Jesus welcomed all of them. Jesus was filled with love for them, because they were like sheep without a shepherd. He taught them about the kingdom of God, and He healed everyone who needed to be healed.

Now it was getting to be late in the day. The disciples said to Jesus, "Send the people away so that they can go into the villages and buy some food to eat. There is no food for them here."

Jesus then said, "You give them something to eat." Jesus asked Philip, "Where should we buy food for all these people?" Jesus knew what He would do but asked Philip this question to test him.

Philip answered, "Even if you worked for eight months, you would not have enough money to give each man even a bite."

Andrew, Simon Peter's brother then said, "Here is a boy who has five loaves of bread and two small fish, but what is that among so many people?"

Jesus told them to have the people sit down on the green grass in groups of 50 and 100. So the people sat down. There were about 5,000 men there, not counting women and children. Jesus took the five loaves and the two fish. Looking up to heaven, He blessed it, thanking God for it. Then Jesus broke it into pieces and gave it to the disciples. They gave it to all the people. Everyone had as much to eat as he wanted.

Then Jesus told the disciples, "Pick up the bread and fish that are left over. None of it should be wasted." When they were finished, there were twelve baskets full of pieces of bread and fish! The people who saw Jesus do many kinds of miracles were amazed and filled with joy. They were sure Jesus was a man sent from God.

The Good Samaritan

(Luke 10)

Many people came to ask Jesus questions, but some only wanted to try and trick Jesus and catch Him saying something wrong. So, quite often, Jesus answered these tricky questions by telling a story. One day one of the religious leaders in Israel came to Jesus and asked, "What must I do to get everlasting life?"

Jesus replied, "What does it say in God's Holy Word?"

The man answered, "Love the Lord your God with all of your heart, and with all of your soul, and all your strength, and all your mind" and to "love your neighbor as yourself."

Jesus said, "You are right. Do this and you will live forever in heaven."

The religious leader wanted to show others how good he was so he asked Jesus, "And who is my neighbor?"

Jesus told this story to answer him.

"A man was traveling from Jerusalem to Jericho. Some robbers were watching. They beat him up and left him beside the road to die. Soon, a priest from the temple in Jerusalem came by. He saw the poor, hurt man but looked the other way and walked on without helping. Not long after came another man who worked in the temple. He also saw the man, but just like the priest, he passed by looking the other way and did not help the man. Now a good man from Samaria came down the road. Jews and people from Samaria never got along and always tried to avoid each other. But the good Samaritan felt sorry for the man who was hurt. He stopped and got off his donkey. The Samaritan bandaged the man's wounds and took him to an inn. He promised to pay whatever it would cost for the man to get well again."

After He had finished the story, Jesus asked, "Tell me, which of these men acted like a good neighbor to the man who was robbed and beaten?" And the religious leader was forced to reply, "The one who helped him, the man from Samaria." Jesus then said, "Then you should also be kind to everyone you meet."

"The good Samaritan felt sorry for the man who was hurt. He stopped and got off his donkey. The Samaritan bandaged the man's wounds and took him to an inn."

In this way Jesus showed a very important lesson through the story of the good Samaritan. We should be like the Samaritan man and show love by being a good neighbor to everybody we meet, not just to our friends and family. We should even help the people who don't like us.

When the Lost Are Found!

(Luke 15)

Jesus told many stories, and people loved to hear them because they were really about God and what God is doing in our lives. Jesus told stories about finding a lost sheep, a missing coin, and a story about a father and his sons.

Jesus said, "A shepherd had one hundred sheep. Every evening, the shepherd carefully counted all his sheep. But one evening, he only counted 99 sheep. So he knew a sheep had wandered away somewhere. The shepherd was sure that he had to leave the 99 sheep and go out to find the missing sheep. The shepherd went out searching in the dark fields. The sun was almost below the horizon, but he went further and further away from home to find the sheep. Suddenly, he heard the sheep calling and rushed to find it.

"He found the sheep, took it and placed it on the back of his shoulders and carried it back home." Jesus then said, "God is like this good shepherd. If someone is lost, God will search and search, find and bring him back again. There is more joy in heaven if one sinner is found and comes back to God and asks for forgiveness, than over 99 other people who did not wander away."

Jesus told another story about the joy there is when something lost is found again. "Imagine a woman who has ten coins and loses one. Won't she light a lamp and clean the house thoroughly, looking in every crack until she finds it?

"And when she finds it you can be sure she will call her friends and neighbors and say: 'Come and celebrate with me! I have found my lost coin!'" Jesus said, "In the same way God's angels are happy when even one person returns to God."

Jesus said, "There was a wealthy man who had two sons. The younger son wanted to leave his father and his home to go someplace far away and enjoy life on his own. So he said, 'Father, give me the money I will get when you die. I want to spend it now!'

"The father was very sad, but he gave the money to him. The young man took the money and went to live far away in another country.

"He made many new friends by inviting them to wild parties all the time. He had a sweet and easy life, but then he ran out of money. Even his new friends left him without giving him any help.

"A great famine came, and the only job he could find was feeding pigs. He was so poor that he wished that he could eat the food he was giving to the pigs. He was miserable. He thought of the wonderful life he had with his father, but so ashamed that he had wasted his father's money, he was afraid to go back home. He said to himself, 'Even the servants of my father have more food than I have here in my misery. I will go back home and ask my father if I can become a servant for him.'

"When he was approaching the house, he could see his father running down the road to meet him. The loving father had been watching every day since his son had left home hoping to see his son come back. The father's heart was filled with great joy when he saw his son.

"My son was dead, and now he is alive again. He was lost, and now he is found!"

"The father hugged and kissed his son. The young man said, 'Father, I have sinned against God and against you. I am not good enough to be your son anymore. Can I be one of the servants here in your house?'

"But the father said, 'No, you cannot be a servant here. You are my son! I am so glad you are finally home again. We shall have a big party and celebrate that my son was lost but has come home to me again.'

"The father then told his servants, 'Kill the fattest calf and make a feast. We will rejoice together. My son was dead, and now he is alive again. He was lost, and now he is found!'

"But the older brother was very angry and refused to come into the feast. His father came to him and encouraged him to come to the celebration. He said to his father, 'I have worked for you all these years. I never disobeyed you, but you never gave me even a young goat to have a little party with my friends. Now this son of yours comes home after he has spent all your money with wild women and parties, and you even killed the fatted calf for him!'

"The father gently said to his son, 'You are always with me, and all that I have is yours. We must celebrate and rejoice. Your brother was dead and is alive. He was lost and now is found.'"

Jesus Heals Many People

(Matthew 15; Mark 7; Luke 17–18)

There was a woman from Syria, who followed Jesus and cried, "Lord, Son of David, please help me. My little girl has an evil spirit that is making her miserable." The disciples tried to make her go away. Jesus told her, "You are not Jewish. I was sent to help the lost sheep of Israel."

The woman begged, "Lord, have mercy on me."

Jesus answered her, "It is not right to take the children's bread and throw it to the puppies."

The woman said to Jesus, "Yes, Lord, but even the puppies eat the crumbs that fall from the master's table." The woman understood that Jesus was the promised Savior of the Jewish people, but she also knew that God's love is for all people.

Jesus said to her, "Woman, you have great faith. I will answer your prayer." At that very time, the evil spirit left her daughter, and she was healed.

Another time there were 10 men at the border of Galilee and Samaria. They all had a sickness called leprosy that made horrible sores all over their bodies. This disease could easily spread to other people. The men had to live outside of the city so that their family and friends did not get the horrible sores. They all called to Jesus and said, "Jesus, Lord, have pity on us."

Jesus said to them, "Go and show yourselves to the priests." The priests would tell them if they could live at home again. As they were on their way to the priests, they were healed, and their skin became clear and healthy again.

One man, as soon as he saw that he was healed, turned around and ran back to Jesus. He praised God with a loud voice and knelt at Jesus' feet to give thanks. This man was from Samaria. Jesus asked, "Didn't all ten men become healthy again? Where are the other nine? Why did only the Samaritan come to give thanks?" Jesus said to him, "Go, your faith has made you well."

As Jesus entered Jericho, there was a blind beggar who called to Him. "Jesus, Son of David, have pity on me." People tried to make him be quiet, but he called louder, "Jesus, Son of David, have mercy on me!"

Jesus told His disciples to bring the man to Him. Jesus asked the man, "What do you want Me to do for you?"

The man answered, "Lord, I want to be able to see."

Jesus said to him, "Receive your sight. Your faith has healed you." The man instantly could see and followed Jesus, giving praise to God. All the people who saw it praised God with him.

Jesus asked, "Didn't all ten men become healthy again? Where are the other nine? Why did only the Samaritan come to give thanks?"

The Good Shepherd

(John 10)

One time Jesus described His love for the people in this way. Jesus said, "I am the Good Shepherd. Any sheep who want to come into the sheep pen must come through Me. I open the door for the sheep who are listening for My voice. My sheep know My voice and follow Me. I know all of My sheep by name, and I call to them. I walk ahead of My sheep, and My sheep follow Me because they know My voice.

"Any sheep that come into My sheep pen will be safe. I will give them life. Robbers try to come into My sheep pen, but My sheep won't listen to them. Robbers and thieves come to steal and kill. I have come so that My sheep will have a good and refreshing life. I am the Good Shepherd, and I will give My own life for My sheep.

"A servant will not take good care of the sheep. He will run away when a wolf comes. He doesn't care if the wolf takes a sheep or makes them run away.

"I take care of My Father's sheep. I am the Good Shepherd. I have other sheep that I will bring into My fold. They will listen to My voice. They will all become one big flock of sheep. I will be the Shepherd of all the sheep. My Father loves Me because I will give My life for all My sheep. I will give My life willingly. I have the power to give it, and I have the power to take My life back again.

"My sheep know My voice, and they follow Me. I will give them everlasting life. They will never be lost, and no one can take My sheep out of My hand."

Jesus was telling the people that He loves them like a shepherd loves his sheep. He has come for all people, not just the Jews. He will give His life for His people and will come alive again. Jesus' sheep will always be safe with Him.

"I am the Good Shepherd.
Any sheep who want to come into the
sheep pen must come through Me.
I open the door for the sheep who
are listening for My voice."

Jesus Loves Children

(John 4; Matthew 18–19; Mark 9–10; Luke 18)

Jesus was deeply concerned for children and showed His special care for them many times. One day an official of the king came to Jesus to ask Him to come heal his son who was dying. The father said, "Lord, come quickly before my little boy dies."

Jesus said, "Go home; your son is now well." The official believed Jesus' words and began his journey home. On the way back, his servants met him. "Your son is well!" they said. "What time did he begin to get better?" asked the father. "The fever left him yesterday at seven o'clock in the morning," they replied. The father remembered that was the time when Jesus said his son would live, and so the father and his family became believers in Jesus. They were so grateful for what Jesus had done for them.

Another time when Jesus returned to His home in Capernaum, He asked the disciples what they had discussed along the way. They were ashamed to admit that they were arguing about who was the greatest among them. Then Jesus called a little child to stand near Him and said, "I tell you the truth, unless you change and become like little children, you will never enter the kingdom of heaven. Humble yourselves like this child. If you welcome a child like this in My name, you welcome Me."

Some people brought little children and babies to Jesus to have Him touch them and pray for them. But Jesus' disciples tried to keep the children away from Him because they thought Jesus was much too busy with more important things and did not have time for small children.

When Jesus heard this, He was very upset with His disciples. Jesus saw them trying to send the children away. He said, "No! You must let these little children come to Me. I tell you this: If you are not going to be like these small children, you will never understand God's kingdom. Let the little children come to Me, for they really belong to God."

Jesus took the children in His arms. He laid His hands on them, and He blessed them.

"If you are not going to be like these small children, you will never understand God's kingdom. Let the little children come to Me, for they really belong to God."

Lazarus, Wake Up!
(Luke 10; John 11-12)

Jesus often visited two sisters living in a town called Bethany. Their names were Martha and Mary. They also had a brother named Lazarus, and one day he became very sick. Therefore they sent a message to Jesus to come and see Lazarus and heal him.

When Jesus heard that His good friend Lazarus was sick, He stayed where He was for 2 more days. Then He said something strange, "Our friend Lazarus has fallen asleep. I will go and wake him up."

The disciples said, "If he is sleeping, he will get better." Jesus meant that Lazarus had died, so He told them plainly, "Lazarus has died. I am glad that I was not there so that you may believe in Me. Now we will go to him."

Some days later, when Jesus came to Bethany, Lazarus' body had been in a tomb for four days. Since the village was only two miles from Jerusalem, many Jews had come to comfort Mary and Martha. Martha ran to meet Jesus, but Mary stayed at home. Martha told Jesus, "Lord, if You had been here, my brother would not have died. Even now, I know that God will do whatever You ask Him."

Jesus said to Martha, "Your brother will rise again." Martha answered, "Yes, Lord, I know that he will rise on the last day." Jesus said, "I am the resurrection and the life. Everyone who believes in Me, even if he dies, will live. Whoever lives and believes in Me will never die. Do you believe this?"

Martha said, "Yes, I believe that You are the promised Savior, God's own Son who has come into the world."

Then Martha went to get Mary. When Mary saw Jesus, she bowed down at His feet, crying, "Lord, if You had been here, my brother Lazarus would not have died."

Lazarus, who had been dead, walked out, alive and perfectly healed. His feet and hands were still wrapped in linen strips.

When Jesus saw her crying, and all those with her also crying, He was filled with sadness. "Where have you laid him?" Jesus asked. "Come and see," they answered. Then Jesus wept. Some said, "See how much Jesus loved Lazarus!"

Others said, "If He could make blind people see, surely He could also have kept Lazarus from dying."

Jesus came to the tomb. It was a cave with a big rock rolled in front. Jesus said, "Roll the stone away!" Martha said, "But Jesus, Lazarus has been dead four days. There will be a horrible smell!"

Jesus told her, "Didn't I tell you that if you believed, you would see what God can do?" When they took the stone away, Jesus looked up and said, "Father, thank You for listening. I know that You always hear Me, but I am saying this so that the people here will believe that You have sent Me."

Jesus then called in a loud voice, "Lazarus, come out!"

When Jesus said this, Lazarus, who had been dead, walked out, alive and perfectly healed. His feet and hands were still wrapped in linen strips. A large cloth covered his face. Jesus said, "Unwrap him. Let him go."

All who saw this were completely astonished to see that God had given Jesus the power to raise Lazarus from the dead. Many of the Jews came to see Jesus when they heard what He had done in Bethany. They also wanted to see Lazarus. The chief priests and the Pharisees started making plans to kill Jesus and plans to kill Lazarus too. They were jealous that so many of the Jews now believed in Jesus, who had the power to bring the dead to life.

227

The Last Days of Jesus in Jerusalem
(Matthew 21-27; Mark 11-14; Luke 19-23; John 12-18)

Jesus knew the time had come to finish God's plan to be our Savior. He traveled to Jerusalem to celebrate Passover with His disciples. Jesus, knowing all that would happen to Him, sent two of His disciples with these instructions: "Go into the village ahead of you. When you enter it, you will find a donkey, and a colt that has never been ridden. Untie them and bring them to Me. If anyone asks you why you are untying them, say, 'The Lord needs them,' and he will send the animals immediately."

The disciples went and found the animals just as the Lord had told them. As they were untying the donkey and colt, the owners said to them, "Why are you untying our colt and donkey?" They replied, "The Lord needs them," and the owners let them take the animals.

The disciples put their coats on the back of the colt, and Jesus sat down on the coats. The disciples gathered around Jesus, and they entered into Jerusalem. Word spread quickly that Jesus had come to Jerusalem, and people ran from everywhere to see Him.

Many of the people laid their cloaks upon the road. Others cut down palm branches and leafy branches from the fields

to spread them on the path. They celebrated Jesus' coming, hoping He would be their new king and throw out the Roman soldiers. They shouted, "Blessed is He who comes in the name of the Lord! Hosanna in the highest!"

On the day that the Passover was celebrated, Jesus sent the two disciples Peter and John into Jerusalem. Jesus said, "Go and prepare the Passover meal for us." "But where shall we prepare it?" Peter asked. Jesus said, "Listen carefully. Go into the city. You will meet a man carrying a water jar. Follow him into the house he enters. Say to the owner of the house, 'The Teacher is asking, "Where is the guest room where I will eat the Passover with My disciples?"' He will then show you a large room upstairs. Just go and make it ready for us." They went and found it exactly as Jesus said it would be and got the room ready.

In the evening Jesus and His disciples met in the room to celebrate the Passover. During the meal Jesus took some of the bread and thanked God for it. While they were eating, Jesus said something strange. "One of you has made an evil plan against Me and is going to help My enemies." The disciples were very surprised to hear this and wondered who could do such a thing. Jesus then took a piece of bread, dipped it in some sauce and handed the bread to Judas. Then He said, "Judas, go and do what you have to do." Judas got up from his seat, left the room, and went into the night. Only Jesus and Judas knew how the evil plan would happen.

As they were eating, Jesus took some of the bread. He blessed it and broke it into pieces and gave some to each disciple. He said, "Take this and eat it. It is My body, given for you. Do this to remember Me." Then, Jesus also took a cup of the wine. He prayed and thanked God for it, and told the disciples to drink some of the wine. Jesus said, "This is My blood. It is a new promise that your sins and the sins of many are forgiven. I cannot be with you much longer and must leave you. When I am no longer here, you should eat bread and drink wine together. When you do this, remember Me and everything I have taught you." Jesus said this because He knew that soon it would be time for Him to suffer and die in Jerusalem, but the disciples could not understand it.

Jesus told them, "I am going to heaven to make a place for you. When I come back, I will take you with Me so that we will be together forever. Do not be afraid. I will send the Holy Spirit to you.

"Blessed is He who comes in the name of the Lord! Hosanna in the highest!"

233

"He will live in you so that you will not be alone. I am going to My Father in heaven, but I will hear you when you pray. If you ask for anything, I will do it for you. Love one another. I have chosen you to be My friends. I will give My life so that you will live forever."

When they had finished the meal, Jesus and His disciples went to a garden called Gethsemane. Jesus knew exactly what would happen to Him. "Please, stay awake and pray with Me this night," Jesus asked them. But the disciples were tired and fell asleep. Jesus was all alone as He went into the middle of the garden to pray. He asked God to make Him brave. An angel came to Jesus to give Him strength.

Judas went to the Jewish leaders and told them where they could find and arrest Jesus. They sent out soldiers, and Judas led them into the garden where Jesus was praying. Judas said, "There will be other men with Jesus, and it is dark and difficult to see who is who. I will walk up to Jesus and kiss Him." In this way the soldiers would know which man they must arrest. When Judas and the soldiers found Jesus in the garden, Judas went straight up to Him and gave Him a kiss on the cheek.

Then the soldiers grabbed Jesus. Peter had seen what was going on, and immediately he drew his sword to protect Jesus from the soldiers. With his sword, Peter hit the servant of the high priest and cut off his ear. Jesus said, "No, Peter, it is not right of you to fight with your sword. I must do what God has planned for Me." Jesus took the ear of the servant and put it back in place and healed him. All of the disciples ran away, and Jesus was arrested by the soldiers.

The soldiers of the temple tied up Jesus and brought Him to be questioned by the Jewish leaders. Caiaphas, the high priest and the whole Jewish council tried to find a law that Jesus had broken that would allow them to kill Him. Finally Caiaphas asked Jesus, "Are you really the promised Savior, the Son of God?"

Jesus said truthfully, "Yes, I am."

But Caiaphas and the other leaders did not believe Jesus. They said to each other, "This man claims to be God's Son, but He is lying. He is just pretending to be God. Now we have a reason to kill Him." Then the Jewish leaders said cruel things to Jesus. They spit on Him and hit Him many times. But the high priest did not have the authority to kill Jesus, so before the sun had even come up, the Jewish leaders brought Jesus to the Roman governor named Pontius Pilate. They wanted Pilate to have Jesus killed. Pontius Pilate went out to speak to them. "What laws has this man broken?"

"If He were not a criminal, we wouldn't have brought Him to you," they said.

"Well, then take Him and judge this man by your own laws," Pontius Pilate said.

But the Jewish leaders said, "We are not allowed to put a man to death. This man makes our people disloyal. He keeps them from paying taxes to Caesar. He says that He is Christ, a king."

Pilate asked Jesus, "Are you the king of the Jews?"

Jesus asked, "I am not a king of this world. I have come into the world to bring the truth."

Pontius Pilate said, "What is truth?" Then he went out and told the Jewish leaders, "I do not find Him guilty of any crime."

But everyone shouted louder and louder, "This man must die! This man must die!" And finally Pilate could not stand the pressure of the big crowd of people who wanted Jesus killed. Pontius Pilate handed Jesus over to them to be crucified. The soldiers took Him, and they led Him away to nail Him on the cross.

When Jesus Died

(Matthew 27; Mark 15; Luke 23; John 18-19)

Jesus carried His own cross as they went out of the city. Soon they grabbed a man from Cyrene, Simon, the father of Alexander and Rufus. They forced Simon to carry the cross for Jesus. A great crowd of people followed them, crying. The soldiers nailed Jesus to the cross outside the city of Jerusalem. Two robbers also hung on crosses. Jesus was in the middle with the criminals on both sides of Him.

A sign was placed above each criminal's head with the reason they were being crucified. On Jesus' sign Pontius Pilate wrote, "Jesus of Nazareth, King of the Jews." The sign was written in Hebrew, Latin, and Greek, so that everyone who passed by could read it.

Then Pilate's soldiers who were keeping watch took Jesus' clothing and divided it up between the four of them. The best item was a robe that was made without a seam, woven from top to bottom. The soldiers said, "Let's not tear it. We can throw lots to see who will get it."

As people walked by the crosses on the way into the city, they made fun of Jesus. The Jewish leaders said, "He saved others, but He can't save himself." "Let Him save Himself if He is the Christ of God, the Chosen One." "Let Him come down off the cross, and then we will believe." "He trusts in God. We will see if God will save Him now."

The soldiers made fun of Him, "If you are the King of the Jews, save yourself!" Even the robber crucified with Him made fun of Jesus. One of the robbers said to Jesus, "Aren't You the promised Savior? Save Yourself and us!"

But the other criminal said, "Aren't you afraid of God, since you are about to die? We are getting the punishment that we deserve. We have done evil things. But this man has done nothing wrong." Then he looked at Jesus and said, "Jesus, remember me when You come into Your kingdom." Jesus promised him, "I tell you the truth. Today you will be with Me in paradise."

Then the sun disappeared, and a great darkness came before Jesus died. Jesus said, "It is finished." Then He breathed His last breath and died. Everyone could see that Jesus was really dead.

Suddenly the curtain in the temple was torn in two from top to bottom. The earth shook, splitting rocks apart. The bodies of holy people, who were asleep in death, were brought back to life. Many people saw them.

When the centurion and men guarding Jesus saw the earthquake and the other things that happened, they were terrified. The centurion said, "This man was innocent. He certainly was the Son of God."

Then the sun disappeared, and a great darkness came before Jesus died. Jesus said, "It is finished." Then He breathed His last breath and died.

We call this very sad day, "Good Friday." It was the saddest day of all because Jesus was really dead. His disciples had forgotten that Jesus told them many times that He would die on the cross. Jesus knew exactly how it would happen. He knew that He would suffer and die because this was God's plan to save His children from the sin and evil that had been brought into the world. When Adam and Eve first disobeyed God, He told them that one of their descendents would crush the devil and save us from our sins. That person was Jesus.

Jesus was kind and good His entire life. He did not do any evil or sin even one time. Because Jesus loves us so much, He allowed the soldiers to nail Him to the cross. Jesus allowed God the Father to punish Him for all of the naughty things and sins that we do. When Jesus died on the cross, God punished Him for the sins of the whole world! Now God is not angry with us. When we do something wrong, we ask Jesus to forgive us and He does! We will live forever with Him in heaven because He promises:

"For God loved the world in this way: He gave His One and Only Son, so that everyone who believes in Him will not perish but have eternal life" (John 3:16).

That is why we call this sad day "Good Friday," but the happiest day of all is about to come . . .

242

The Resurrection of Jesus

(Matthew 28; Mark 16; Luke 24; John 20; 1 Peter 3)

There was a rich man named Joseph, from Arimathea. He was a respected member of the Jewish council but had not agreed to their evil plan to kill Jesus. In fact he was a secret disciple of Jesus. Joseph went to Pontius Pilate and asked for the body of Jesus. Pilate was surprised that Jesus was already dead. He ordered that Jesus' body be given to Joseph so he could bury Him.

Joseph brought a linen burial cloth and took Jesus' body down from the cross. Then they took Him to a garden nearby where there was a tomb that had been cut out of the rock. The tomb belonged to Joseph. They wrapped Jesus' body in the cloth. Then they rolled a stone against the entrance of the tomb and went home.

On Saturday, the chief priests and Pharisees met. They all went to speak to Pontius Pilate. "Sir, we remember that when this liar was still alive He said, 'In three days I will come alive again.' Give the order to guard the tomb until after the third day. Otherwise His disciples will come and steal His body and say to the people, 'See, He has risen from the dead.' Then this trick will be worse than the first."

Pontius Pilate said to them, "You have soldiers that can serve as guards. Send them to watch the tomb and make it as secure as you can." So the chief priests sent soldiers to guard the tomb. They sealed the stone to make sure no one rolled the stone away.

Early in the morning, the third day after Jesus died, suddenly, there was a great earthquake. An angel from God came down from heaven, rolled the stone away, and sat on it. He was shining as bright as lightning. His clothes were as white as snow! The temple guards were so terrified that they shook and became like dead men. Jesus was no longer dead. He was alive again. God had brought Jesus back to life!

A little later that same morning, the two disciples Peter and John and a woman named Mary Magdalene came to see the cave where Jesus had been buried. When they came near the tomb, they could see that the big stone had been rolled away. Jesus was no longer there. The grave was empty! Peter went inside the cave and found cloth that had been wrapped around Jesus' body. The piece of cloth that had been wrapped around Jesus' head was neatly folded beside it.

Mary Magdalene also entered and went inside the cave. She saw two angels. One of them said to her, "Why are you looking for Jesus here? Jesus is no longer here. He has risen from the dead and is alive again just like He told you."

Mary came out of the cave. When she turned around, she saw Jesus standing there, but she did not know who He was. Jesus asked her, "Why are you crying? Who are you looking for?"

Mary thought He was the gardener and said, "Sir, if you have taken His body away, please tell me so I can go and get Him." Then Jesus said to her, "Mary." Finally, Mary realized Jesus was standing right beside her and that He was alive again. She hugged Him tightly. Jesus said, "Go and tell My brothers, "I am returning to My Father and your Father, to My God and your God." Then she went back to tell everybody the wonderful news.

"Jesus is no longer here. He has risen from the dead and is alive again just like He told you."

Jesus Appears to His Disciples

(Mark 16; Luke 24; John 20)

Mary Magdalene ran to the disciples and told them what she had seen. She told them that she had hugged Jesus, but they did not believe her. Even when Mary told them what Jesus had said, they still did not believe her.

That very night, Jesus appeared to His disciples. They had locked the door, but suddenly Jesus appeared to them. "Peace be with you!" Jesus said. The disciples were very frightened. They thought that Jesus was a ghost!

Jesus said to them, "Why are you afraid? Why do you doubt what you see? Look at My hands and feet. See! It is really Me! Touch Me and see for yourselves! A ghost does not have muscles and bones, but you can see that I do!"

The disciples looked at Jesus' hands and feet. They were so amazed and excited that they could not believe it. Jesus asked them,

"Do you have anything here to eat?" They gave Him a piece of broiled fish and watched Him eat it.

He said to them, "Don't you remember what I told you when I was with you? I had to do everything that was written about Me in God's Holy Word, everything that was written about Me by Moses and the prophets, and in the Psalms.

Then Jesus helped them understand God's Holy Word. He explained that everything He had done proved that He was really the Savior.

He said, "This is what God's Word says, 'The Savior will suffer and rise from the dead on the third day. The people will be told to be sorry for their sins and ask to be forgiven in His name. All the people in the whole world will hear this starting in Jerusalem.' You are my witnesses, and I will send you a special gift that My Father has promised."

Then Jesus breathed on them and said to them, "Receive the Holy Spirit. If

you forgive anyone's sins, they will be forgiven. If you do not forgive them, they will not be forgiven."

Thomas was not there that night. When the other disciples told him, "We have seen the Lord!" Thomas did not believe them. He said, "Unless I see the nail marks in His hands and put my finger in there, I will not believe it."

The doors were locked again, but Jesus appeared to them and said, "Peace be to you." He said to Thomas, "Put your finger into the nail holes in My hands. Stop doubting and believe!" Thomas said, "My Lord and my God."

Jesus said, "Now that you have seen Me, you believe. Blessings will be given to the people who have not seen Me and still believe."

251

Big Catch of Fish

(John 21)

One night not long after Jesus had died and been brought back to life again by God, the disciples went out fishing. Simon Peter said, "I am going fishing." "We'll go with you," said the other disciples, and immediately they got into the boat. They fished all night but did not catch anything.

Just as the sun was coming up, Jesus stood on the shore, but they didn't recognize Him. He called to them and said, "Boys, do you have any fish?" "No," they answered.

"Throw your net on the right side of the boat, and you will find some," Jesus said to them.

The disciples obeyed and dropped the net into the water on the other side of the boat. When they pulled up the net again, it was heavy with fish. It was truly a miracle! John then said to Peter, "I am sure that must be Jesus!" When Peter heard this, he put his robe back on and jumped into the sea. The other disciples brought in the boat, dragging the net full of fish.

When they all arrived on shore, they saw burning coals cooking fish and also some bread. Jesus said to them, "Bring some of the fish that you just caught." Peter got back into the small boat and helped pull the net to shore. There were 153 big fish in the net! Although there were so many fish, the net was not even torn! Jesus said, "Now come and have breakfast." Jesus Himself gave them the bread and also the fish to eat.

Jesus wanted to spend some time with the disciples. He wanted to show that even though they could not always see Him, He was still with them and would take care of them. Now they must be ready for their new job of teaching others about God. This was the third time that Jesus showed Himself to the disciples since He had risen from the dead.

Jesus Returns to Heaven
(Luke 24; Acts 1-2; 1 Corinthians 15)

During the 40 days after Jesus rose from the dead, He appeared to many people. Jesus even appeared to over 500 people who were gathered together at the same time. While He was in Galilee, Jesus told His disciples, "Go and make more disciples of people everywhere. Baptize them in the name of the Father and of the Son and of the Holy Spirit. Teach them to do all that I have taught you. I will be with you always to the end of time." Jesus knew it was time for Him to return to heaven. So, Jesus took His disciples to a hill outside of Jerusalem.

Jesus said, "It's time for Me to go back to heaven to be with my Father. After I'm back in heaven, you must go back to Jerusalem and wait there until I send My Spirit to you. After that you will go out everywhere in the world to tell people about Me and everything I have taught you during these years we have spent together."

As He was talking to them, Jesus began to rise up to heaven. The disciples stared, looking up, as Jesus went higher and higher into the sky. Then a cloud hid Him from their sight. For a long time, the disciples stood silently and looked up into the sky. They did not know what to think and say about this. They didn't understand that Jesus had to go back to heaven to be with God. Suddenly two men dressed in white shining clothes stood right next to them. The angels asked, "Why are you standing here looking up in the sky? Jesus has gone to heaven, and one day Jesus will come back to Earth again the same way you have now seen Him leave Earth." The disciples knelt and worshipped Jesus. The disciples then returned to Jerusalem with a happy heart waiting for God's Holy Spirit to be sent to them just like Jesus had promised.

"Why are you standing here looking up in the sky? Jesus has gone to heaven, and one day Jesus will come back to Earth again the same way you have now seen Him leave Earth."

Several days later, it was the day of Pentecost. The disciples were gathered at one place in Jerusalem close to the big temple. The temple was filled with people because it was a very special holiday. Every year Jews from all over the world traveled to Jerusalem to celebrate this holiday in the temple where the people thanked God for the wonderful blessings He had given to them in the harvest.

Suddenly there was a loud noise. It sounded like a mighty wind. Then they saw little flames of fire that looked like tongues in the air above their heads. They were all filled with the Holy Spirit. The Holy Spirit gave them power to speak in languages they had never learned before. The Holy Spirit was the gift Jesus had promised His disciples when He went back up to heaven. The Holy Spirit gave the disciples courage and the right words to tell everyone in the whole world about Jesus.

People rushed over to see what was going on. Even though the people had come from many countries, they all could understand what the disciples were telling them about God and Jesus in their own language. God had given the disciples very special powers this day. Everyone was amazed that the disciples were suddenly able to speak in languages they had never learned. People were surprised and wondered what it meant.

But some also made fun of them, saying, "They have had too much wine."

Peter then stood up and said, "Fellow Jews, all who live in Jerusalem, let me explain this to you. These men are not drunk. It is only nine in the morning. It is by God's Holy Spirit that these men speak in new languages. I tell you that Jesus of Nazareth, whom you crucified, was God's Son. He was betrayed and killed by you, but it was according to the exact plans made by God. You killed Jesus by nailing Him to a cross! But on the third day, God raised Him up, and death has no longer any power over Jesus. He is alive again and has returned to heaven to be with God. Let everyone in Israel understand this: God made Jesus, whom you crucified, both Lord and Christ."

When many of the people heard this, they mmediately knew in their hearts that Peter was telling the truth. They asked Peter and the other disciples, "Brothers, what can we do now?" Peter answered, "Be sorry and turn from your sins.

Be baptized, every one of you, in the name of Jesus Christ, so that you will be forgiven of your sins and receive the Holy Spirit. This promise is for you and your children, for everyone in the whole world."

All those who believed what Peter had preached were baptized, and more than 3,000 people became Christians on that day. The new Christians were helping the disciples as much they could. They shared in worship, eating, and praying together. Everyone was amazed by all of the miracles done by the disciples. They all shared their belongings, even selling their belongings to give to those who had need. Every day they met in the temple courts to study and praise God. God blessed them, and the first church was growing as every day more new believers became Christians.

God's Wonderful City– Our True Home!

(Revelation 1; 4; 7; 21-22)

The disciple John, always called himself, "the disciple whom Jesus loved." He wrote many letters to different churches all over the world. John lived longer than any of the other disciples and became a very old man. John spent all his life telling about Jesus. He traveled to faraway countries. The wonderful message of Jesus and how He died to save us from our sins reached to the farthest places on earth. The other disciples had also spent their lives preaching the good news about Jesus. Now people everywhere were talking about Jesus and trusting that He was their Savior.

Late in his life, John was forced to stay on a small island called Patmos. The enemies of Christians hoped he would no longer be able to speak of the good news of Jesus' death and resurrection. But God had special plans for John.

One day Jesus came and appeared to John in a vision. In this very special experience, John was suddenly able to see right into heaven, where God is. Jesus was showing him what would happen in the future.

John saw Jesus dressed in a splendid white robe, and he saw God seated on His throne surrounded by many angels. He saw a great number of people from every nation, from all tribes and peoples and languages, dressed in white robes. They were holding palm branches and worshipping God, saying, "Holy, holy, holy is God the Almighty."

Later John saw a new heaven and a new earth. God was making His home with His people. They will be His people, and He will be with them always. He will wipe away every tear from their eyes. There will be no more death, sickness, crying, grief, or pain. John wrote down all of what he saw and heard. Then, John sent letters about it to his friends so they could tell other Christians about what he had seen and been told about the future.

There will be a big beautiful city with streets like polished gold and buildings made of shimmering gold and glass. In the middle of the city, there is a beautiful river and along the river are trees. The most wonderful fruits are growing on these trees. Every month there is a different fruit, and when people eat the fruit, they live forever.

It will never be night in heaven. God's children will not need a light or the sun because God Himself will be the light and shine on us. Only good and wonderful things happen there. The most wonderful and amazing thing is that God, our Father, and Jesus will live there with us forever. Jesus is waiting for us to be there with Him when we leave this world. He is preparing a home for us, and there is plenty of room for everyone.

Jesus is waiting for us to be there with Him when we leave this world. He is preparing a home for us, and there is plenty of room for everyone.

The Apostles' Creed

This has been used for hundreds of years and is still used today by Christians around the world to teach and confess the Christian faith.

I believe in God, the Father Almighty,
maker of heaven and earth.

And in Jesus Christ, His only Son, our Lord,
who was conceived by the Holy Spirit,
born of the virgin Mary,
suffered under Pontius Pilate,
was crucified, died, and was buried.
He descended into hell.
On the third day He rose again from the dead.
He ascended into heaven
and sits on the right hand of God the Father Almighty.
From thence He will come to judge the living and the dead.

I believe in the Holy Spirit,
the holy Christian Church,
the communion of saints,
the forgiveness of sins,
the resurrection of the body,
and the life everlasting.
Amen.